Improving the Adoption of Software Engineering Practices Through Persuasive Interventions

Von der Fakultät für Elektrotechnik und Informatik
der Gottfried Wilhelm Leibniz Universität Hannover
zur Erlangung des Grades

Doktor der Naturwissenschaften
Dr. rer. nat.

genehmigte Dissertation

von

M. Sc. Leif-Gerrit Singer

geboren am 16. September 1979 in Hannover

2013

Referent: Prof. Dr. Kurt Schneider
Korreferent: Prof. Dr. Arie van Deursen
Tag der Promotion: 11. Februar 2013

Für Claudi und Iven.

Leif Singer. *Improving the Adoption of Software Engineering Practices Through Persuasive Interventions*. PhD thesis, Gottfried Wilhelm Leibniz Universität Hannover, 2013.

ISBN 978-1-291-27311-3

Acknowledgments

This thesis would not have been possible — or, at least, would have been *less* possible — without the support from many others. They taught, helped, and challenged me in various ways and contributed to my development in one way or another.

I am deeply grateful to my parents. They supported me in my endeavors, even though some of them might not have seemed too useful back then.

Stefan, thanks for your fearless, hands-on approach to learning. I can't possibly say how much that helped me finding my way.

I thank my advisor, Prof. Dr. Kurt Schneider, for first providing me with advice and so many opportunities, and then, later, the freedom to develop and to work on what I felt passionate about. I thank my second examiner, Arie van Deursen, for his challenging comments.

I thank my local colleagues for a great workplace. Especially Olga and Raphael: thank you for a fun, energetic office. Sebastian, thank you for your companionship over the years. Daniel, I'm still grateful for your mentorship, especially during the studies for my Master's.

Throughout my studies, I got to know so many interesting and kind researchers — some of them in person, some only remotely. I'm deeply grateful to you all for making me feel so welcome in this community.

I thank those who participated in our experiment, interviews, and questionnaires. The kindness and generosity of complete strangers delight me again and again. I'm especially thankful to Vanessa Ramos of Masterbranch and Matthew Deiters of Coderwall, who both supported the study documented in section 5.3.

Thank you, Claudi, for your ongoing support and understanding. Without you, this would not have been possible and certainly less worthwhile. Finally, Iven — you might not have understood much of what was going on during these days, but your enthusiasm helped me getting through the rougher ones.

Hannover, February 2013   *Leif Singer*

Abstract

Software engineering practices and methodologies are not always adopted by software developers, even if these approaches are mandated by the developers' organization. Research has uncovered different reasons for this: for example, missing motivation, peer pressure, perceived usefulness, or perceived complexity can all prevent developers from successfully adopting a practice or methodology. However, software engineering practices and methodologies can have a significant positive impact on software quality and developer productivity: for example, pair programming can lead to improvements in code correctness, and the use of design patterns can improve developers' productivity as well as reduce defects. Issues with adoption can therefore have a negative impact on a software development organization.

Most research in this area has concentrated on explaining adoption problems. Among the findings originating from this research is the insight that mandating a behavior alone cannot solve adoption problems. Solution approaches should instead augment the mandating of practices to include other factors that are important for the diffusion of innovations. Such factors include social influence, knowledge management, motivation, and persuasion.

This thesis proposes such an approach to improve the adoption of software engineering practices by software developers. As an augmentation to mandating practices, it uses persuasive — i.e., non-coercive — software-based interventions that can facilitate creativity, autonomy, and other crucial factors in software development. To support organizations in designing such interventions, the thesis provides a catalog of *adoption patterns*: abstract solutions to adoption problems. A systematic and iterative process provides guidance in the application of these patterns to the organization's situation. An evaluation of this approach shows that the process and the adoption patterns are effective: for student developers, a significant improvement in their application of best practices for version control was achieved.

Improving the adoption of software engineering practices in a supportive, non-coercive manner may not only have a positive impact on the time, costs, and quality of software development projects. According to prior research, such an approach can also support employee satisfaction, productivity, and retention.

Keywords: software engineering, best practices, adoption, diffusion of innovations, motivation, social media, social software, persuasive technology, coercion.

Zusammenfassung

Praktiken und Methodiken des Software Engineering werden nicht immer von Entwicklern übernommen, selbst wenn diese vorgeschrieben sind. Bisherige Forschung hat hierfür verschiedene Gründe aufgedeckt: fehlende Motivation, Druck von Kollegen, die wahrgenommene Nützlichkeit, oder auch die wahrgenommene Komplexität können Entwickler davon abhalten, Praktiken zu übernehmen. Allerdings können diese einen positiven Einfluss auf die Qualität von Software und die Produktivität von Entwicklern haben: bspw. kann Pair Programming zu korrekterem Code führen; Design Patterns können die Produktivität erhöhen und Fehler reduzieren. Probleme mit der Übernahme von Praktiken können daher Unternehmen negativ beeinflussen.

Ein Großteil der Forschung hat sich auf die Gründe und mögliche Modelle für Übernahmeprobleme im Software Engineering konzentriert. So wurde herausgefunden, dass das Vorschreiben von Praktiken alleine derartige Probleme nicht lösen kann. Lösungen sollten stattdessen andere Faktoren miteinbeziehen, die für die Verbreitung von Ideen und Praktiken wichtig sind: so etwa soziale Beeinflussung, Wissensmanagement, Motivation und Überzeugungsstrategien.

Diese Dissertation schlägt einen solchen Ansatz vor. Als Ergänzung zum Vor-schreiben von Praktiken verwendet er software-basierte "überzeugende" (engl.: *persuasive*) Interventionen, die Kreativität, Autonomie und andere in der Softwareentwicklung wichtige Faktoren begünstigen können. Um Organisationen beim Entwurf solcher Interventionen zu unterstützen, bietet die Dissertation einen Katalog von *Übernahme-Mustern*: abstrakte Lösungen zu Übernahmeproblemen. Ein systematischer, iterativer Prozess unterstützt dabei, Muster auf die jeweilige Situation einer Organisation anzuwenden. Eine Evaluierung dieses Ansatzes zeigt, dass Prozess und Muster effektiv sind: für Studierende der Informatik konnte eine signifikante Verbesserung der Übernahme von Praktiken zur Versionskontrolle gezeigt werden.

Die Verbesserung der Übernahmen von Praktiken des Software Engineering auf unterstützende und überzeugende Art kann nicht nur auf Zeit,

Kosten und Softwarequalität einen positiven Einfluss haben. Laut Forschung sollte ein solcher Ansatz auch die Zufriedenheit und Produktivität von Mitarbeitern verbessern und deren Verbleiben im Unternehmen begünstigen.

Schlagwörter: Software Engineering, Best Practice, Übernahme, Verbreitung von Innovationen, Motivation, Social Media, Social Software, überzeugende Technologie, Zwang.

Contents

1. Introduction

The adoption of software engineering practices by members of an organization can have a significant impact on the productivity of software developers and the quality of the software they develop. To facilitate the adoption of such practices, this thesis contributes a catalog of adoption patterns extracted from prior research, as well as a process that provides a systematic procedure for applying these patterns.

This chapter introduces the addressed problem, sketches the proposed solution, defines the scope of this thesis' contributions, and provides an overview of the research methods used.

1.1. Motivation

Software engineering practices, tools, and methodologies — if used correctly — can have a positive influence on the quality and costs of developed software and on software development processes themselves. For example, Oram and Wilson [132] present a collection of empirical evidence regarding practices such as test-driven development, pair programming, code reviews, modularization, and design patterns.

In practice, however, developers do not always apply these practices — even if they are mandated by their organization and would be helpful. This has been shown in several studies (e.g. Riemenschneider et al. [146], Hardgrave et al. [84], Fitzgerald [61]). For software development organizations, such developer resistance can for example lead to failure in deploying software process improvement (SPI) initiatives [146], lessening or nullifying the expected positive impact of such initiatives.

1.2. Approach

To mitigate developer resistance and its impacts, this thesis investigates alternatives to prescribing the use of practices, tools, and methodologies. To guide this effort, Rogers' [149] model of the diffusion of innovations is used as a theoretical background. Rogers shows that apart from prescribing the adoption of a practice, several other strategies and factors are important to achieve diffusion in a population — e.g., among the software developers of an organization [149].

As Storey et al. [169] point out, social media bear potential for having a strong impact on software development, some of which has already been realized. Therefore, diffusion of innovations theory is augmented with results from empirical studies that investigated the influences of social media on developers' adoption of practices and technologies. Based on the results of these studies and an extensive literature review in diverse fields, this thesis contributes a process and a catalog of adoption patterns. These can be used in organizations to improve the adoption of software engineering practices in a persuasive, i.e., non-coercive manner. The process and the pattern catalog are evaluated in a quasi-experiment[1], showing that significant improvements in practice adoption can be achieved with relatively simple, but systematically constructed persuasive interventions.

1.3. Scope & Assumptions

This section discusses the scope of this thesis and its assumptions.

1.3.1. Scope

Software interventions The persuasive interventions proposed by this thesis consist of treatments that are realized as software applications. Several other interventions can be useful for behavior change — e.g. meetings, discussions, monetary rewards or punishments (cf. e.g. Geller et al. [70]). However, these are out this thesis' scope.

Persuasion Non-persuasive strategies to influence practice adoption, such as coercion, psychological pressure, or punishment can be implemented in software [62]. However, as Amabile and Kramer [6] show, such approaches are suboptimal — especially for creative professions like software engineering. Therefore, this thesis is restricted to approaches that support creativity and collaboration through *persuasion*, a non-coercive approach to behavior change.

---

[1]In a quasi-experiment, the assignment of subjects to the control vs. treatment conditions is non-random.

Interventions do not change practices   To improve the adoption of software engineering practices, this thesis proposes the deployment of persuasive interventions. The intent of these interventions is not to change the practices themselves. Rather, they influence the interactions between developers and the interactions of developers with the practices. While other results might be achievable by optimizing the practices themselves for adoption processes, such an approach is not covered by this thesis.

Society   This thesis uses research results from psychology, e.g. in the literature review that is used to derive the adoption patterns. As Henrich et al. [85] have shown, study results in psychology often only apply to a very small subset of the human population: individuals living in *"Western, Educated, Industrialized, Rich, and Democratic (WEIRD)"* societies. Therefore, the mechanisms used by the adoption patterns might not be applicable to individuals from other societies.

1.3.2. Assumptions

Suitability of practices   This thesis does not make any assumptions about the suitability or effectiveness of the software engineering practices that an organization has chosen for adoption. However, several adoption patterns will be difficult to apply for unsuitable or ineffective practices, as they may rely on, for example, communicating the value a practice creates for the colleagues of a developer.

Co-location and distribution   Social media and mechanisms associated with it can be used for distributed software development, in which developer teams may be working in different countries, time zones, and cultures [100]. However, the approach presented in this thesis does not address this distinction. Instead, it assumes that the adoption patterns may work in distributed as well as in co-located development. This is supported by observation like those by Bertram et al. [15]: they find that software support often associated with distributed development can be beneficial for co-located development as well.

Organizational change   Organizations provide stability for their members. While this is beneficial in several aspects, one consequence of stability is that change becomes harder [149]. This may hamper the adoption of practices and the efforts that support adoption processes. However, this thesis assumes that an organization has already decided to adopt a certain practice. The presented approach is therefore concerned with the individual innovation-decision process [149].

Methodologies consist of practices Developers may resist the adoption of individual practices as well as whole methodologies. In the context of this thesis, it is assumed that improving the adoption of individual practices can also improve the adoption of a methodology.

Capability This thesis assumes that individuals and organizations are *capable* of introducing interventions as described in later chapters, and that individual developers are *capable* of applying the prescribed software engineering practices correctly. The process and patterns presented in this thesis are concerned with factors other than capability — such as persuasion and motivation.

1.4. Research Methods

To investigate the influences of social media mechanisms on software developers, I collaborated with colleagues in two empirical studies (cf. sections 5.2 and 5.3). In both studies, we conducted exploratory research guided by Grounded Theory [170]. Based on Creswell's recommendations [33], we chose different mixed methods designs.

Empirical Study: Testing on GitHub Using testing as an example for a software engineering practice, we investigated the influence of social media — namely, the social coding site GitHub — on the adoption of practices. In this study (cf. section 5.2), we used Grounded Theory as our research method [170]. Grounded Theory is a method for qualitative research that originated in sociology. It suggests an iterative approach in which qualitative data is collected and analyzed in parallel. Using open coding, selective coding, and axial coding, researchers extract common themes from their data, relate them to each other, and create an overarching theory with one of the themes at its core.

In this study, we started with a qualitative phase consisting of semi-structured interviews to determine our research questions. This was followed by a first questionnaire that supported narrowing our questions even further. We then proceeded with a second round of semi-structured interviews, this time directly aimed at answering our more concrete research questions. As suggested by Greiler et al. [79], we validated our qualitative results with a second questionnaire.

Empirical Study: Mutual Assessment in Social Media for Developers In a more general study on the influence of social media on software developers (cf. section 5.3), we started with a set of more concrete research questions. This allowed us to begin with a questionnaire targeted at members of two social media sites for developers, which supplied us with first quantitative results. We extended on those with semi-structured interviews, yielding qualitative insights. For this qualitative phase, we again used Grounded Theory.

Process and Patterns To construct a process (cf. chapter 6) and a catalog of patterns to support this process (cf. chapter 7), I conducted an extensive literature review of the effects social media can have on adoption processes. As these can be found in different fields such as HCI, software engineering, psychology, and sociology, a systematic literature review as proposed by Kitchenham [92] was not appropriate. For the same reason, a systematic literature survey (cf. e.g. Cornelissen et al. [31]) also was not an option. To construct the process and the patterns from the literature review's results, I used open and selective coding as e.g. suggested by Grounded Theory [170].

Quasi-Experiment: Version Control Practices in a Student Project To evaluate the process and the patterns, I applied them to a student project (cf. chapter 8). In this quasi-experiment, the control group consisted of the reasonably similar past projects. For the treatment group, a persuasive intervention — constructed based on the process and adoption patterns contributed by this thesis — was deployed. In the treatment condition, student developers committed significantly more often to version control, and wrote more and longer commit messages.

In summary, the research presented in this thesis is based on a problem identified in literature, empirical studies of a possible solution approach, the construction of a concrete solution based on a literature review, and a quasi-experiment validating this solution.

1.5. Structure

This thesis is structured as follows. The following three chapters provide the backgrounds for research on the *Diffusion of Innovations*, *Self-Determination Theory* — a model of human motivation —, and *computer-supported cooperative work*. Chapter 5 gives an overview of adoption challenges and solutions in software engineering, and reports on two studies on this topic I conducted in cooperation with other researchers. The succeeding chapter describes a process for influencing practice adoption; chapter 7 documents the patterns for this process that I derived from literature. Chapter 8 reports on a quasi-experiment that shows the effectiveness of the approach. Chapter 9 discusses related work, and chapter 10 concludes the thesis and considers areas for future research.

2. Diffusion of Innovations

This chapter introduces the theory of the diffusion of innovations [149]. It provides the theoretical background for this thesis. Based on this theory, later chapters develop a solution targeted at improving the adoption of software engineering practices.

2.1. Elements

Rogers [149] defines *diffusion* as follows.

Definition 1: Diffusion.

"Diffusion is the process by which an innovation *is communicated through certain* channels *over* time *among the members of a* social system.*"*

(cf. Rogers [149])

This section introduces the terminology used in that definition.

Definition 2: Innovation.

"An innovation is an idea, practice, or object that is perceived as new by an individual or other unit of adoption."

(cf. Rogers [149])

Rogers emphasizes the *perception* of newness — in discussing the diffusion of innovations, it is irrelevant whether an innovation is truly novel.

Innovations are diffused through communication channels:

Definition 3: Communication Channel.

"A communication channel is the means by which messages get from one individual to another."

(cf. Rogers [149])

Many different kinds of communication channels exist, and each may have different properties with regard to the diffusion of innovations through them. Yet, first and foremost, Rogers identifies two distinct classes of channels: mass media and interpersonal channels. Mass media broadcast messages — such as news, educational information, or TV shows — from a sender to many receivers. Conversely, interpersonal channels exist between individuals and allow for exchanges between them that can go back and forth.

While mass media are initially important to spread awareness knowledge about an innovation, interpersonal networks become more important with time as people turn to their peers for opinions about and evaluations of an innovation.

Time, which determines the ordering of events, is also an important aspect of the diffusion of innovations. Diffusion is a process that unfolds over time. Thus, time is relevant when investigating how an individual or other unit of adoption gradually changes their internal state (e.g. knowledge or decision to adopt) and overt behavior (actual adoption or rejection). Time is also an important measure when categorizing adopters into different categories (cf. section 2.3) or when determining an innovation's *rate of adoption* — the number of adopters for an innovation in a given period [149].

Finally, diffusion always happens within a social system.

Definition 4: Social System.

"A social system *is defined as a set of interrelated units that are engaged in joint problem solving to accomplish a common goal. The members or units of a social system may be individuals, informal groups, organizations, and/or subsystems."*

(cf. Rogers [149])

For social systems, diffusion research distinguishes between two different structures. The *social structure* influences diffusion through values, norms, roles, and hierarchies. Furthermore, the *communication structure* determines how messages may flow through the social system, e.g. by providing communication links between individuals. Because of their influences on the diffusion process, both structures are of interest for diffusion researchers [149].

2.2. The Innovation-Decision Process

The *innovation-decision process* describes how individuals — or other decision-making units, such as groups or communities — adopt or reject an innovation. This process is aimed at reducing the uncertainty about an innovation. It is comprised of five steps (cf. Fig. 2.3) that do not necessarily need to follow each other consecutively [149].

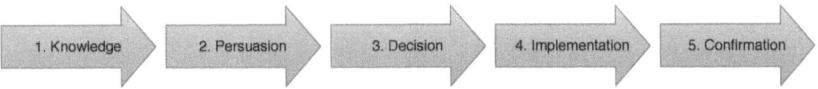

Figure 2.1: *The innovation-decision process for individuals according to Rogers [149].*

1. *Knowledge:* The individual becomes aware of the innovation's existence and starts to understand how it works.

   For example, a software developer might learn about test-driven development (TDD) by reading about it in a blog post.

2. *Persuasion:* The individual develops an attitude towards an innovation.

   Through a discussion with a colleague that was triggered by the blog post, the software developer realizes that using TDD could be beneficial in her development.

3. *Decision:* An individual who is aware of an innovation and has formed an attitude towards it will at some point decide whether to adopt the innovation. This often involves a trial phase by the individual herself or by a peer.

   After the discussion with the colleague, the developer contemplating TDD for her development tries a tutorial she finds on the Web and then decides to start applying TDD from now on.

4. *Implementation:* The individual starts using the innovation. She continues learning about it and overcomes problems, further reducing the innovation's uncertainty.

   The software developer now uses TDD in her daily work and keeps informing herself to improve her application of TDD, for example through exchanges with colleagues who have also adopted TDD.

5. *Confirmation:* After having implemented an innovation, an adopter will continue to collect information that reinforces her decision. If this leads to conflicting information, the adoption may be reversed.

The software developer will constantly monitor herself and her peers to reinforce or refute whether adopting TDD actually does improve the process of developing software in some way.

The passive or active consumption of awareness knowledge and how-to knowledge, the opinions of peers, and personal trials all help a potential adopter in this process. By gradually improving her understanding of an innovation, she reduces the uncertainty associated with ideas perceived as new. Each stage in this process bears the potential for the individual to reject the innovation, e.g. by forgetting about it after the knowledge stage or by not acting upon their positive attitude towards the innovation [149].

2.2.1. The KAP-Gap

The latter phenomenon is called the knowledge-attitude-practice gap (KAP-gap). It describes the situation in which individuals have gained awareness knowledge and how-to knowledge about an innovation, have formed a favorable attitude towards it, but do not act upon it. It often occurs for *preventive innovations*: those which can prevent or mitigate an undesirable future event. Because the effect of adopting the innovation is a "non-event" — something *not* happening — the benefits of the innovation are not as accessible as for other innovations [149]. An example for software engineering is writing documentation to prevent problems during maintenance: as it is not clear whether there will be maintenance problems or whether the developer will be involved in maintenance at all, she may perceive documentation as unnecessary overhead [102].

By connecting Rogers' theory with social learning theory [9] (cf. section 2.5.3) and self-determination theory [150] (cf. chapter 3), motivation can be derived as one factor determining whether an individual will reject an innovation in the KAP-gap. Bandura acknowledges that motivation is an important part in social learning [9], without which individuals will not reproduce the behavior they have observed. Relatedly, according to Ryan and Deci [150], motivation is necessary to apply existing skills or learn news ones. Therefore, this thesis assumes motivation to play a role for overcoming the KAP-gap.

2.3. Adopter Categories

Based the findings of several studies, Rogers [149] uses a measure of "innovativeness" to distinguish different categories of adopters. Using the average time of adoption for a population and an individual's time of adoption, the individual can be associated with one of the following five adopter categories. Boundaries between categories are based on standard deviations from the average time of adoption (cf. Fig. 2.2).

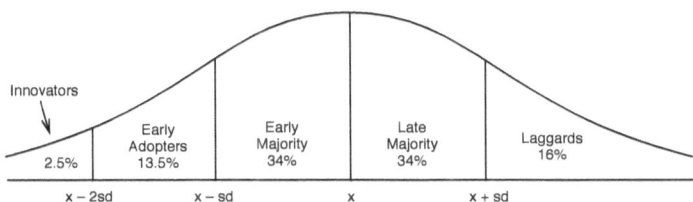

Figure 2.2: *Rogers' proposed categorization of adopters based on the average time to adopt (x) and the standard deviation (sd) [149].*

Rogers [149] ascribes different characteristics to each adopter category:

1. ***Innovators:*** Innovators are venturesome and interested in new ideas. They are less connected to their local peer networks, and keep more cosmopolite relationships with other innovators that might be geographically distanced. To support their affinity for novelty, uncertainty, and risk, they need sufficient financial resources, must be able to understand technical concepts, and need to be able to cope with uncertainty.

   Innovators play an important role in the diffusion of innovations. Their cosmopolite relationships, especially those to other innovations, allow them to import new ideas into their local peer networks. This makes them gatekeepers that have control over the flow of innovations between social systems.

2. ***Early Adopters:*** Compared to the innovators, early adopters are oriented more towards their local peer networks. They are respected by their peers, who often refer to them for advice and information about an innovation.

   Early adopters serve as role models for other members of a social system. Once they have adopted an innovation, they communicate their evaluation of it to their peers, who use this evaluation to reduce their own uncertainty about an innovation. Through this process, early adopters can support an innovation in reaching the critical mass that enables the innovation to become adopted more widely.

3. **Early Majority:** A third of the adopters in a social system are in the early majority. They adopt new ideas just before the average member does.

   While they do not lead adoption and do not serve as opinion leaders, their interconnectedness in the social system makes them an important link in the diffusion of innovations.

4. **Late Majority:** Just as the early majority, the late majority constitutes a third of the adopters in a social system. They adopt new ideas after the average member has done so. Their reasons for adoption are often economic necessity or increasing peer pressure.

   Because of their lower resources, members of the late majority are skeptical about innovations: they need to be sure that the investment will be worthwhile.

5. **Laggards:** Laggards are oriented towards the past and use it as a reference for their decisions. They interact with peers who are similarly traditional as themselves, isolating them from the rest of their social system.

   The laggards' cautious adoption behavior is often based on their limited resources. Before they adopt an innovation, they need to be sure that it will not fail.

Rogers [149] notes that these are *ideal types*, and that reality shows a continuous spectrum of adopters over time. However, they are a useful abstraction for thinking about the process of diffusion.

As the adopter categories show, an individual's personal situation and characteristics can influence their *time of adoption*. Similarly, the next section shows how attributes of innovations themselves can determine their *rate of adoption*.

2.4. Attributes of Innovations

Rogers identifies five attributes of innovations that have a strong influence on whether and how fast an innovation is adopted. He notes that these need not be *actual* attributes of an innovation — it is only important how a potential adopter *perceives* the innovation [149].

1. *Relative Advantage:* The perceived relative advantage of an innovation is the degree to which it is perceived as improving on a previous innovation. This can manifest itself as higher profitability or an increase in social status, for example. *Preventive innovations* — those whose effects may not be immediately visible, or may never materialize because their purpose is to prevent an undesirable event — are perceived to have a very low relative advantage. Incentives (e.g. money or free samples) can be used to increase the perceived relative advantage of an innovation. However, adoptions motivated by incentives may be less sustainable, with adopters possibly rejecting the innovation when the incentive ceases to be available. Relative advantage is positively related to an innovation's rate of adoption.

2. *Compatibility:* The perceived compatibility of an innovation describes how consistent it is with regard to an individual's values, experiences, and needs. The degree of compatibility determines the change in behavior required to adopt an innovation. Thus, instead of introducing an incompatible innovation into a social system, adoption can be easier when the innovation is broken up into several more compatible innovations that can be adopted in sequence — each requiring only a minor behavior change. Compatibility is positively related to an innovation's rate of adoption.

3. *Complexity:* The perceived complexity of an innovation describes how difficult it seems to comprehend and use the innovation. A high degree of complexity can be a strong barrier against adoption. Complexity is negatively related to an innovation's rate of adoption.

4. *Trialability:* The perceived trialability of an innovation is the degree to which it can be tried on a probationary basis. A personal trial of an innovation is an effective way to reduce uncertainty about an innovation. As such, trialability is positively related to an innovation's rate of adoption.

5. **Observability:** The perceived observability of an innovation is the degree to which others can observe the results of an innovation. Observing a peer can be a proxy for a trial of an innovation. Observability is positively related to an innovation's rate of adoption.

These five attributes have been found to determine about half of the variance of adoption rates [149].

2.5. Diffusion Networks

The adoption rate is also influenced by the social system in which an innovation diffuses. Rogers mentions *weak ties, opinion leaders, social learning,* and *critical mass* as important concepts that help understand the diffusion of innovations through social networks [149].

As has been alluded to in the section on adopter categories, many individuals are influenced by peers when deciding whether or not to adopt an innovation. Peers from distant social networks introduce innovators to new ideas. This gatekeeping process gives the relatively locally oriented early adopters access to these innovations. Acting as opinion leaders, they demonstrate the advantages of an innovation to the early majority. Through peer pressure and out of economic necessity, the late majority and laggards finally also adopt the innovation. The diffusion process of an innovation is driven by interpersonal communication.

2.5.1. Weak Ties

Research has shown that with high probability, an individual's close ties are similar to the individual (cf. a discussion on homophily by McPherson et al. [119]). These peers, in turn, are peers to one another as well. This gives rise to mostly isolated, close-knit cliques. Consequently, new ideas are unlikely to enter such a social system [149].

However, some individuals in such groups will have ties to individuals from other communities. Because they belong to other peer groups, such connections are often weaker. Yet, these *weak ties* [78] provide the means for seeding peer networks with innovations. They act as brokers that bridge communities and allow new ideas to flow from one peer group to another.

Thus, while most ties between individuals have a low potential for the exchange of new ideas, the rare and distant weak ties can act as impactful channels in the diffusion of innovations. Close, strong ties are more important when it comes to interpersonal influence [149].

2.5.2. Opinion Leaders

For illustrative purposes, Rogers' theory divides individuals into *opinion leaders* and their *followers*, acknowledging that in reality, this distinction is not as clear-cut [149].

Opinion leaders have exposure to mass media and are cosmopolite. They participate more in their social systems than their followers and have a higher socioeconomic status. Often, opinion leaders are more innovative than their followers — but this depends on whether the social system favors change [149].

These characteristics give opinion leaders immense influence when it comes to diffusing innovations in a social system. Because their opinions are highly respected, their followers often find them more credible than external influences such as mass media or change agents. For this reason, change agents often seek opinion leaders in a social system to help them diffuse an innovation. Rogers cites several studies that have shown that this approach is more effective than alternatives — like, e.g., simply trying to communicate an innovation to *all* members of a social system [149].

The observability of an innovation is an important attribute in this regard, as demonstrations by opinion leaders can be impressive "trials by proxy" for a potential adopter [149].

2.5.3. Social Learning Theory

Bandura [9] introduced social learning theory to explain how individuals learn from each other's behavior by observations. This process is called social modeling: based on observing peers, individuals enact similar — not identical — behavior. Instead of imitating others, they adapt an observed behavior to their own situation. If the original behavior leads to an observable reward for the original performer, others can take this as a cue to start modeling their own behavior after the original. Social modeling can happen through interpersonal networks as well as through public displays, for example through mass media. The steps Bandura regards as necessary for social learning to happen include attention (the ability to observe a behavior), retention (remembering a behavior), reproduction (i.e., ability to perform a behavior), and motivation.

Social learning and the diffusion of innovations are distinct theories. Yet, they are related in that they both provide a model of behavior change based on communication with others. Both theories regard information exchange an essential factor in behavior change, and both acknowledge ties between individuals as an important facilitator of such exchanges [149].

2.5.4. Critical Mass

Critical mass for an innovation is the point at which its diffusion becomes self-sustaining and does not need to be supported by change agents or similar forces anymore [149]. It is especially important for *interactive innovations*: Rogers defines these as innovations through which an exchange between individuals is facilitated, and which allow individuals to switch roles. Examples are many communications technologies, like the telephone, fax, email, or social media sites. They have in common that with each additional adoption, the value of adopting the innovation increases for all past and future adopters [149].

Since potential adopters are often aware of the fact that the innovation will be more useful if others adopt it, they monitor the adoption behavior of others. Individuals will be more likely to adopt if they perceive that critical mass has been reached, as this increases the innovation's value. Relatedly, opinion leaders are often part of the critical mass, as they are watched by their followers [149].

Conversely, if an individual believes that others are discontinuing their adoption of an interactive innovation, they will also be more likely to stop using it: discontinuance for such an innovation is equivalent to a decrease in value. This can create cascades of discontinuance that will eventually lead to the innovation becoming abandoned [149].

Rogers [149] proposes four strategies to support an innovation in reaching critical mass: targeting highly-respected individuals for initial adoption; shaping the *perceptions* of whether critical mass will be reached soon or has already been reached; introducing the innovation first to especially innovative groups, such as R&D departments; and providing incentives for early adoption until critical mass is reached.

2.6. The Organizational Innovation Process

This thesis is concerned with influencing *individual* developers in their adoption of software engineering practices. However, as the approach presented in this thesis assumes that developers work in the context of an organization, this section briefly discusses the innovation process for organizations (cf. Fig. 2.3). According to Rogers [149], it is comprised of the following steps.

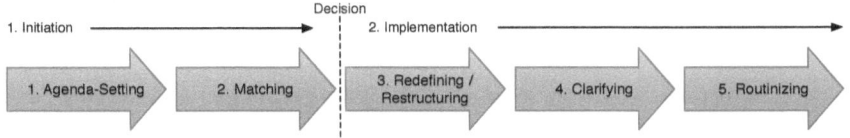

Figure 2.3: *The innovation process for organizations according to Rogers [149].*

1. ***Agenda-Setting:*** The organization identifies and prioritizes needs and problems that could be addressed by adopting an innovation.

2. ***Matching:*** The problem identified in the previous stage is matched with an innovation that could solve it.

3. ***Redefining / Restructuring:*** The organization customizes the innovation according to its own structure, culture, and needs.

4. ***Clarifying:*** Use of the innovation is starting to diffuse in the organization. The meaning of the innovation becomes clearer for the organization's members, and they start forming a common understanding of it.

5. ***Routinizing:*** The innovation loses its distinct quality: it is now part of the organization.

This thesis assumes that an organization has already decided about adopting a certain practice and that the problem lies with the adoption of individual developers. Therefore, only the *clarifying* and *routinizing* stages from the above process will be relevant.

2.7. Diffusion of Innovations and Software Engineering

Iivari [87] discusses the apparent non-use of computer-aided software engineering (CASE) tools in organizations. Whereas reported effects of CASE tool usage on software quality were beneficial, the adoption of such tools was found to be low. For example, the author cites a study showing that 70% of CASE tools deployed in organizations were not used after one year. Iivari uses Rogers' diffusion of innovations theory [149] to examine this phenomenon. He interprets his findings to show that CASE usage could be increased by stronger management support, encouragement, and by making it mandatory. This would initiate a self-sustaining cycle in which perceived relative advantage would increase as developers gain experience with CASE tools, which would further improve adoption.

Iivari's discussion supports this thesis' assumption that *some* mandating of behavior supports the adoption of software engineering innovations, but that perceived attributes of innovations such as relative advantage can be leveraged to improve the adoption of software engineering innovations even further.

A workshop series on adoption-centric software engineering (ACSE, c.f. e.g. Balzer et al. [8]) that was successfully organized over several years highlights the importance of addressing adoption problems in software engineering research.

2.8. Summary

During the process of diffusion, an innovation is communicated through communication channels among the members of a social system. The innovation-decision process describes the stages an individual can go through while contemplating the adoption of an innovation: after having gained knowledge about it, the individual forms an opinion about the innovation and decides whether or not to adopt it. The individual then starts using the innovation and further reduces the remaining uncertainty by practice and learning. When the innovation has been adopted, the individual continues to monitor whether adoption still makes sense for her.

Adopters as well as attributes of innovations can be divided into categories established by diffusion research. Their characteristics can provide an estimate of the probability of adoption in a given situation. Social networks have a large influence on the adoption process.

As section 2.2.1 has argued, motivation can be an important factor when an individual considers an innovation for adoption. The next chapter discusses Self-determination Theory — a model of human motivation. This will clarify challenges and possible solutions to improving the adoption for software engineering practices.

3. Self-determination Theory

Self-determination Theory (SDT) is a macro theory of human motivation. As described in the previous chapter, developer motivation can have an impact on their completion of the innovation-decision process — namely in the KAP-gap, between the persuasion and decision stages. This chapter provides an overview of SDT to guide the design of persuasive interventions for improving the adoption of software engineering practices in later chapters.

Research in psychology has created many models of human motivation. SDT is a model that has been confirmed by current research and is accepted in the psychology community (cf. e.g. Deci and Ryan [44]). Gagné and Deci [68] have shown that SDT also applies to work settings, making it suitable for supporting software engineers.

3.1. Basic Psychological Needs

According to Ryan and Deci [151], the base assumption of SDT is that human beings "have natural, innate, and constructive tendencies to develop an ever more elaborated and unified sense of self." That is, when sufficiently supported, people will strive "to learn; extend themselves; invest effort; master new skills; and apply their talents responsibly." [150]

However, when missing the necessary support, individuals can become fragmented, passive, reactive, or alienated [151]. Ryan and Deci acknowledge three fundamental psychological needs that need to be satisfied for an individual to thrive.

1. **Competence:** Competence refers to individuals feeling effective in their interactions with their environments and experience exercising and expressing their capacities. The competence need is related to seeking attainable challenges that match and extend one's capabilities [151].

2. **Relatedness:** Relatedness refers to individuals feeling "connected to others, to caring for and being cared for by those others", and

to a feeling of belonging [151]. It is related to feeling secure in the company of one's peers.

3. **Autonomy:** Autonomy "refers to being the perceived origin or source of one's own behavior." [151] Contrary to intuition, the autonomy need is not related to independence. Rather, it refers to individuals' need of feeling in control of their environment and their actions.

These three basic needs can be supported by various strategies. For example, encountering challenges that are both attainable, yet stretch an individual's capabilities to a new level, can support perceived competence [151]. Unexpected positive feedback on these challenges also supports perceived competence [43], while negative feedback can thwart it, leading to lowered intrinsic motivation [184]. Csíkszentmihályi's concept of the *flow experience* is related to the autonomy and competence needs [35]. The autonomy need can be supported by giving individuals choice in their tasks [198].

3.2. Intrinsic & Extrinsic Motivation

Self-determination Theory distinguishes between two different kinds of motivation: intrinsic and extrinsic motivation. Individuals that are intrinsically motivated to carry out a task do so because of the enjoyment or fulfillment that are, in their perception, inherent to the task. Conversely, extrinsic motivation is external to the task itself: individuals perform the task to reach another goal, such as obtaining a reward, avoiding punishment, or gaining in social status.

3.2.1. Intrinsic Motivation

To explain intrinsic motivation, Self-determination Theory contains Cognitive Evaluation Theory (CET) as a sub-theory [151]. CET does not specify what *causes* intrinsic motivation — rather, Ryan and Deci view it as having evolved in humans. Instead, CET is concerned with factors that can support or inhibit an individual's natural potential for intrinsic motivation.

The most important supporting factors for intrinsic motivation are perceived autonomy and competence. Both must be present for intrinsic motivation to thrive [150]. Facilitators for perceived competence are, for example, optimal challenges, positive performance feedback, and freedom from demeaning evaluations [150]. At the same time, the individual must experience her behavior as self-determined, i.e., experience autonomy. Relatedness can further support intrinsic motivations [150].

The sustainability of engaging in an activity, productivity, and the well-being of individuals are associated with motivations that are more intrinsic [150]. This especially applies to creative activities — as opposed to routine work, for which extrinsic motivators such as rewards can provide legitimate support. Whereas intrinsic motivation can lead to higher and more sustained engagement with a creative activity, extrinsic motivation can facilitate engagement in routine tasks that are not intrinsically rewarding, or push individuals to try out a behavior they have not performed before.

3.2.2. Extrinsic Motivation and Internalization

For understanding extrinsic motivation, Self-determination Theory provides another sub-theory: Organismic Integration Theory (OIT) [150].

Extrinsic motivators — such as rewards or deadlines — can motivate an individual to perform a task she is not intrinsically motivated to do. However, if the individual *is* intrinsically motivated for the task, extrinsic motivators can *diminish* that existing motivation. When rewards, threats, directives, deadlines, pressured evaluations, or imposed goals are present for a task, the person ceases performing it for its own sake and loses her sense of autonomy. Expected extrinsic motivators undermine intrinsic motivation. Thus, if the extrinsic motivator is then removed, the individual might stop performing the behavior [150].

However, not all extrinsic motivators are the same: OIT recognizes a continuum that distinguishes extrinsic motivations based on how internalized the motivation is for the individual and on the degree of perceived autonomy [150] (cf. Fig. 3.1).

The different nuances of motivation (Fig. 3.1) have been shown to have different influences on individuals [150]:

1. **Amotivation:** Individuals who are amotivated do not act or merely act without intent. It can be caused by "not valuing an activity, not feeling competent to do it, or not expecting it to yield a desired outcome." [150]

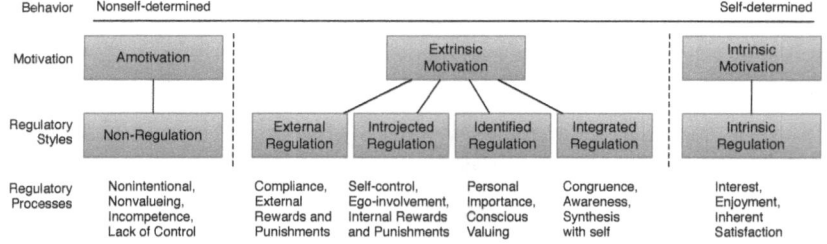

Figure 3.1: *The different types of motivation as according to Self-determination Theory [150].*

A bored software tester mindlessly clicking through user interface dialogs and possibly making mistakes doing is an example for amotivated behavior.

2. ***Extrinsic motivation, external regulation:*** Behaviors that are externally regulated are performed "to satisfy an external demand" or because of the possibility of a reward. Individuals experience it as controlled or alienated [150].

When a software developer is writing her lines of code only because she will earn 10 Euros for each 100 lines, she is extrinsically motivated with external regulation.

3. ***Extrinsic motivation, introjected regulation:*** Introjected behaviors "are performed to avoid guilt or anxiety or to attain ego enhancements such as pride." The behavior is not experienced as part of oneself, but as externally influenced [150].

For example, a software developer who is working on a task only to avoid disappointing her team is extrinsically motivated with introjected regulation.

4. ***Extrinsic motivation, identified regulation:*** For identified behaviors, the action is "accepted or owned as personally important". The individual consciously values the goal or regulation [150].

An example for identified regulation is a software developer who is fixing a bug not because she enjoys doing it, but because she acknowledges that it is necessary to move the project forward.

5. ***Extrinsic motivation, integrated regulation:*** If identified regulators become part of the self — that is, the individual has evaluated them and was able to align them with her own values — they are called *integrated* [150].

   When a software developer is performing an unattractive task because she knows that practicing this task will make her a better developer, she is extrinsically motivated with integrated regulation.

6. ***Intrinsic motivation:*** An individual performs an activity only for the sake of the activity itself, feeling autonomous and self-determined [150].

Activities that are more internalized are associated with greater initiative, better coping with failure, less anxiety, more enjoyment, more effort, and better performance [150]. Arguably, these are desirable qualities for creative work like software development. Therefore, to support software engineers' motivation to help them overcome the KAP-gap, facilitating the internalization of extrinsic motivations is desirable.

Influences from others — e.g. colleagues or superiors — are the main reason individuals engage in activities they are not intrinsically motivated for. Supporting perceived relatedness, therefore, is a crucial element when facilitating the internalization of extrinsic motivators [150]. Similar findings hold for feelings of competence and autonomy. People are more likely to adopt a behavior when they feel capable of performing it [150], and supporting autonomy by providing individuals a sense of choice and freedom from external pressures "allows individuals to actively transform values into their own." [150]

Chapters 6 and 7 will incorporate these insights when developing a process and adoption patterns that can improve the adoption of software engineering practices — including by helping developers overcome the KAP-gap with motivational support.

3.3. Motivation and Software Engineering

The influence of motivation on software development has long been acknowledged in software engineering research and practice. However, empirical research is rare. This section gives examples for some mentions and investigations of related phenomena.

In his 1981 book *Software Engineering Economics*, Barry Boehm [16] discusses the influence of developer motivation on productivity. He advises managers of software development projects to especially support the growth needs of their developers, as "for many software people, a good deal of self-actualization is involved with becoming a better software professional." (p. 670) Boehm also warns of some simple strategies that seem to increase productivity, but do so only in the short term. For example, he criticizes reducing software development tasks into small, meaningless pieces, or using planning and control metrics — extrinsic motivators — for performance-appraisal (pp. 645, 638). Boehm also mentions the detrimental effect of low motivation on employee retention.

In their 1987 book *Peopleware*, DeMarco and Lister [46] discuss several issues of motivation in software engineering. The authors criticize the use of extrinsic motivators ("management [means] kicking ass") as being infeasible for the software engineering profession, as such approaches are unlikely to produce creative, innovative work and will unlikely be sustainable in the long run. Instead, DeMarco and Lister argue that software engineers "love their work" and that extrinsic motivation from management is "almost always superfluous".

A recent study by Sach et al. [153] supports that software engineering itself is a motivating task. In a subsequent investigation, Sach and Petre [152] find support for the beneficial impact of positive feedback and the detrimental effect of negative feedback, a theme mentioned earlier in this chapter.

Beecham et al. [12] conducted a systematic literature review on motivation in software engineering. They find that software engineers are more interested in growth (i.e., challenges and learning) than in achievements (e.g. promotions) and that they value independence. According the authors, motivated engineers tend to stay in their jobs longer and are more productive than de-motivated ones.

Finally, McConnell [118] points out that since motivation is a soft factor that is hard to quantify, software development organizations often ignore it, concentrating on more measurable aspects they can influence.

3.4. Summary

SDT as a *model* of human motivation may not contain the whole truth about what motivates human beings. However, it is a useful model and, according to research, works well in explaining behavior and creating solutions. Therefore, it is also appropriate for guiding the design of software engineering practices and supporting tools to put them more in line with what motivates developers — helping them overcome the KAP-gap.

As the previous chapter has shown, interpersonal networks play an important role in the diffusion of innovations. The next chapter discusses how these can be supported in software. Mechanisms from such applications can then be used to design persuasive interventions that improve the adoption of software engineering practices.

4. Computer-supported Cooperative Work

Software developers use computers not only for writing programs — they also use them to communicate and collaborate with one another. Software development is an inherently social activity: collaboration and communication activities can have a powerful impact on the success of software projects (cf. e.g. Stapel and Schneider [166]). Computer-support for these activities is not restricted to distributed projects, in which necessity requires computer-mediated communication. Instead, even co-located teams use software that supports group communication and collaboration in their daily work [15].

This thesis develops *adoption patterns* — abstract solutions to adoption problems — to improve the adoption of software engineering practices (cf. chapter 7). Many of these adoption patterns leverage mechanisms that improve collaboration and communication of software developers. To enable a better understanding of how and why these patterns work, this chapter provides a summary of some relevant topics from the field of computer-supported cooperative work (CSCW).

4.1. Introduction

The first mention of using a computer for human interaction was in 1945, in Vannevar Bush's essay *As We May Think* [23]. The author describes a device he calls the *memex*. The memex provides access to a large encyclopedia that humans can influence and shape, allowing them to exchange data with another. Another milestone publication is an article by Licklider and Taylor [104] from 1968, in which the authors describe how a computer can be used for communication.

CSCW is a line of research concerned with how social interactions — communication, collaboration, or coordination — are influenced by technical systems. In the 1970s, it became clear that computers were needed to support collaboration. However, research in computer science and software engineering was not yet prepared to answer what the requirements for such a system should be. Knowing how to build software was not enough

— some understanding of how people interact and collaborate was missing. In this situation, Irene Greif and Paul Cashman organized a *CSCW* workshop, which would coin the term CSCW for a discipline that works in understanding such requirements [80]. Whereas research in this area is referred to as CSCW, the technology and systems that implement CSCW concepts are often called *groupware* [80].

4.1.1. Groupware

Ellis et al. [54] define groupware as follows:

Definition 5: Groupware.

"Computer-based systems that support groups of people engaged in a common task (or goal) and that provide an interface to a shared environment" are called groupware.

(cf. [54])

According to the authors, the goal of groupware is to support communication, collaboration, and coordination for groups of people.

The above definition of groupware does not provide a clear-cut differentiator. Instead, groupware is regarded as a continuum along multiple dimensions, two of which are the *common task* and the *shared workspace*. These dimensions can be used to classify an application on the groupware spectrum. For example, because of missing environmental cues, email is considered to be *low* on the groupware spectrum. Conversely, a collaborative text editor is *high* on the groupware spectrum, as it supports a group achieving a common task: creating, editing, or reviewing a document [54].

Grudin [80] mentions the organization as the largest entity that could be the subject of CSCW, respectively groupware. However, since his definition, another type of systems has emerged that is also relevant to CSCW research: social media, which often encompass whole communities and are not focused on supporting their users to achieve a *common* task.

4.1.2. Social Media

To allow for a definition of social media, definition 6 first defines what media are.

> **Definition 6: Media.**
>
> Media *are storage and transmission channels or tools used to store and deliver information or data.*
>
> *(cf. Merriam-Webster Online Dictionary [1])*

Social media, then, are those media that allow exchanges *between large numbers of users* (cf. definition 7).

> **Definition 7: Social Media.**
>
> Social Media *are media that allow large numbers of users to share content with one another.*

Modern social media are often implemented as web sites, but not always[1]. Kietzmann et al. [90] provide an overview of the functional building blocks that can be found in social media, noting that not every social media site will contain every building block:

1. *Identity* lets users disclose information about themselves to other users.

2. *Conversations* support communication between users of the social medium.

3. *Sharing* allows users to exchange, distribute, and receive content.

4. *Presence* enables users to know how accessible another users is — e.g. with regard to their geographical location or the task they are currently working on.

5. *Relationships* allow users to create connections between themselves that are persisted in the social medium.

6. *Reputation* lets users estimate others' and their own standing among their peers.

7. *Groups* allow users to form sub-communities.

---

[1]E.g. users of Instagram primarily access the service through an application for smartphones http://instagr.am

Social media are available for a variety of purposes. For example, content repositories allow users to exchange a certain type of content — e.g. music, videos, or photographs — with one another. Flickr[2] is an example for a content repository for photographs. Microblogs, such as Twitter[3], let users post short texts in a public space. Question & answer (Q&A) sites (e.g. Stack Overflow[4]) let users post and answer questions, sometimes focused on a specific topic. Social network sites (SNS) like Facebook[5] are focused on letting users create relationships between each other (cf. definition 8). Social coding sites such as GitHub[6] are a combination of content repositories and social network sites targeted at software developers.

Social network sites are particular, as their defining features can be added to any other social media site. Ellison and boyd [55] define SNS as follows.

Definition 8: Social Network Site.

"A social network site is a networked communication platform in which participants 1) have uniquely identifiable profiles that consist of user-supplied content, content provided by other users, and/or system-provided data; 2) can publicly articulate connections that can be viewed and traversed by others; and 3) can consume, produce, and/or interact with streams of user-generated content provided by their connections on the site."

(cf. Ellison and boyd [55])

Thus, from the examples mentioned before, GitHub *is* a social network site: members of the site have a profile; they can follow other users and inspect whom another user follows; and they are provided with a stream of updates from users and projects they follow on the site. Whereas Stack Overflow, the Q&A site for software developers, does not allow persistent connections between users. Thus, Stack Overflow *is not* a social network site.

---

[2]http://flickr.com
[3]https://twitter.com
[4]http://stackoverflow.com
[5]http://facebook.com
[6]http://github.com

4.2. Modeling Social Cues

When creating groupware, social media, or related systems, it is important to appropriately support social processes [80]. One set of approaches to this is concerned with modeling social cues — signals that are taken for granted in interactions that take place in the physical world, but are not available by default when interacting through computer systems. For example, colleagues who are co-located in an office room and are working on reorganizing the chapters of a book by physically rearranging hard copies will notice when one of them picks up a chapter. This allows them to react, for example by preventing the colleague to do so because they think the change would be inappropriate. This section presents research areas that are concerned with making such social cues explicit in computer systems.

4.2.1. Awareness

In supporting communication, collaboration, and coordination, *awareness* support has become an important tool. Dourish and Bellotti [51] first defined it as "an understanding of the activities of others, which provides a context for your own activity." Today, CSCW distinguishes the following different types of awareness [105]:

- **Group awareness** informs members of a collaborating team about what other members are working on and what their current status is.

- **Workspace awareness** refers to information about a team's shared workspace, often presented in a spatial manner. This can include artifacts, their editing histories, and the availability of team members.

- **Contextual awareness** can be provided in *addition*: based on the current context, it filters the available awareness information to contain only that which is relevant to the user in their current context (e.g. their location, current task, or most closely worked with colleagues).

- **Peripheral awareness** — similar to contextual awareness — refers not to an additional kind of awareness information, but to a way of displaying existing information. A system supporting peripheral awareness displays awareness information not as a central entity, but in the *periphery* of a user's workspace, allowing them to concentrate on their current task, but providing a space to switch to for awareness information.

Many modern awareness systems automatically collect and publish awareness information about an individual. Therefore, a recurring issue is the amount of awareness information a system should provide. Too much information could overwhelm users, but too little information might cease to be useful. For example, Wang et al. [190] as well as Shah and Marchionini [161] find that this is a trade-off that must be balanced for each application and kind of task. The authors propose methods to appropriately tailor awareness information.

4.2.2. Social Translucence

To choose which social cues to model in a system and how to represent them, Erickson et al. [57, 56] argue that the physical world should be the reference. This is where humans have evolved their capabilities to interpret social signals, therefore computer systems should be designed so that these capabilities can assist users of computer systems as well. This approach is called *social translucence*, referring to making social cues *visible*, but hiding others that would disturb the users' goals.

Erickson et al. [57, 56] distinguish three aspects in their approach: *visibility* makes social cues explicit; this creates *awareness*; and awareness, in turn, creates *accountability*. Relating to the example about rearranging book chapters above, making the act of picking up a book chapter chapter *visible* would make colleagues *aware* of it. The colleague picking up the chapter would know that her colleagues are aware of it, creating *accountability*.

Social Translucence Over Social Networks

Social translucence was created with the physical world as the ideal space after which to model computer system. However, according to Gilbert [71], this approach breaks down in social media and on social network sites. These systems are structured by their users' social networks — the connections between them — which have no equivalent in the physical world.

Even though this allows these systems to scale[7], it also creates problems that cannot easily be addressed by social translucence.

Gilbert provides an extension of social translucence that allows addressing such problems even when social networks are used to structure group communication. His approach, for now, is based on a consideration of *triads* in social networks — relationships between three actors, in this case as a directed graph. By listing the possible configurations and examining them with regard to one of the three traits from social translucence (visibility; awareness; accountability), Gilbert is able to discover design problems that have not yet been addressed [71].

4.2.3. Social Transparency

As another approach to address the shortcomings of social translucence with regard to social media, Stuart et al. [171] created their *social transparency* framework. It is a theoretical framework that can guide the design and analysis of software systems through which individuals communicate, collaborate, or coordinate. The authors identify three dimensions of transparency that can be used to increase or decrease the perceived degree of transparency of a system. Changes in each of the dimensions can affect the social processes supported by a system in several ways.

- *Identity Transparency* is the degree to which the identity of the participants of an information exchange is visible to other participants. Users might be completely anonymous, identifiable only by nicknames, or by their real names. Reputation signals may help in identifying the credibility of a participant.

  For example, software developers use identity cues present in social media to assess each other, informing their decisions of whether to initiate a collaboration or not [162].

- *Content Transparency* refers to "the visibility of the origin and history of actions taken on information." [171] That is, for content in a software system, it describes the degree to which the recipient can determine the source of the content, which states it was in before, and which users were responsible for these states.

---

[7]e.g., Twitter had 100 million active users in September 2011: http://blog.twitter.com/2011/09/one-hundred-million-voices.html; Facebook had 1 billion active users as of October 2012: http://newsroom.fb.com/Key-Facts

For example, the social coding site GitHub displays all prior versions of an artifact and connects them to the users responsible for them.

- **Interaction Transparency** is the degree to which information exchanges between a sender and a receiver can be observed by a third party.

  For example, Twitter users are able to passively follow exchanges between other users they follow.

Different degrees of transparency in these three dimensions can have diverse effects. For example, users that have to use their real names in a software system will feel more accountable for their actions, but might also be more reluctant to post controversial opinions. Receivers of content will interpret information differently based on where it came from, so the presence or absence of reputation signals will influence the credibility of a source.

In addition to such first order effects, *second order effects* — i.e., effects of effects — complicate the targeted application of transparency. For example, if the popularity of information and information sources is transparent, a community of users may tend to prefer only popular content, thereby silencing niche opinions.

Among these effects, it has been shown that the motivations and behaviors of a system's users can be influenced positively. For example, users of social network sites are more likely to engage in a behavior if they have observed their peers exhibiting the behavior before [22, 26]. Publicly visible extrinsic rewards such as badges or public ranking lists can motivate developers to try out new practices and technologies [162]. The process and several of the adoption patterns proposed by this thesis (cf. chapters 6 and 7) provide a systematic way to leverage such effects of social transparency to improve the adoption of software engineering practices.

4.3. CSCW in Software Engineering

This section discusses existing approaches from software engineering that utilize the modeling of social cues in collaboration systems to support software development.

4.3.1. Groupware

Several features known from groupware and mentioned above are present in collaboration tools for software engineering. This section highlights some examples.

Awareness support in distributed development Steinmacher et al. [168] conducted a systematic literature review about awareness support for distributed software development. They find that collaboration tools supporting awareness features are becoming more numerous. Coordination is supported by the most tools, a communication focus however is less prominent. Workspace awareness elements play a central role in distributed software development.

Awareness through dashboards and feeds In an industrial study by Treude et al. [180], the authors investigate the use of dashboards and feeds in software development. They find that these tools increase awareness in projects. Dashboards support individual as well as collective processes. Feeds are rather used to track work at a small scale.

Trust in distributed teams Because of cultural differences, distributed teams encounter challenges in building up trust. Even though it can build up in the co-located teams of a distributed project's sites, trust *between* sites can be hard to achieve. According to Mikawa et al. [121], informal conversations and spontaneous brainstorming are some key factors that support building up trust, but are not supported by the often task-driven collaboration tools. For example, developers will only initiate video conferences to achieve certain goals, leaving no room for informal talk that could support inter-site trust. As was described in previous sections, such informal communication can be facilitated by modeling social cues.

Collaboration tools for distributed development Lanubile et al. [100] provide an overview of collaboration tools used in global software engineering. While they mention the important part social media can play in facilitating informal communication, they also present several more traditional collaboration tools. The authors discuss web-based tools for requirements engineering, software design, and testing — demonstrating that collaboration tools exist for many areas of software engineering.

Stakeholder involvement for requirements engineering   Lohmann et al. [109] created a Web platform to support requirements engineering activities. Namely, their system implements several features known from social media to increase stakeholders' engagement in requirements engineering. As it is targeted at the earlier stages of requirements gathering and discussion, the system uses social media features such as commenting and rating to especially foster informal exchanges.

Conflict detection and notifications for coordination   Brun et al. [21] present a tool that can detect possible collaboration conflicts in version control repositories. When the tool detects a new commit from another developer that could create a conflict with the work of the tool's user, it provides a warning. This workspace awareness enables software developers to avoid conflicts in using version control.

Peripheral visualizations for coordination   Lanza et al. [101] present a set of visualization that provide awareness information to developers. Similar to the approach by Brun et al. [21], their tool enables developers to become aware of possible merge conflicts in a shared codebase. However, instead of technically detecting possible conflicts, Lanza et al. provide visualizations that are present in developers' peripheral workspace at all times. These visualizations allow developers to realize when someone else is working on the same code, and according to a qualitative study are effective in prompting discussion between developers — thereby avoiding complicated merge conflicts.

Expert discovery based on source code involvement   Guzzi and Begel [81] present CARES, a collaboration tool integrated into the IDE that helps software developers find and communicate with experts on the source code they are currently working on. The authors find that their tool makes it easier and faster for developers to find and contact others who might be able to help them with a problem. This was especially the case when developers did not know whom they should contact.

Communication and knowledge management in issue trackers   Bertram et al. [15] investigated the use of issue trackers in co-located software development. According to the authors, issue trackers are used to communicate and coordinate work with involvement from diverse stakeholders, such as customers, project managers, quality assurance, and the developers themselves. Even though the primary use case for an issue tracker seems to be tracking defects and providing prioritized task lists, Bertram et al. find that they serve as important repositories of organizational knowledge.

4.3.2. Social Media

Social media have changed how developers create software. Software engineers connect with, provide help to, collaborate with, and learn from one another with unprecedented ease [169]. Relatedly, Begel et al. [13] show that social media can support team processes in software engineering. This section gives examples of social media use in software engineering.

Collaborative documentation Wikis [39] and blogs [134, 133] were among the first social media that were used by software developers. They are mostly used for requirements engineering, documentation, and to communicate high-level concepts [112, 3, 169]. Blogs and Q&A sites facilitate collaborate learning and augment official API documentation [136].

Question & answer sites Stack Overflow is a question & answer site targeted at software developers. Members can post questions, provide answers and comments, and rate both questions and answers. The site uses *gamification* concepts — *"the use of game design elements in non-game contexts"* [50] — to encourage and reward participation. Remarkably, a question asked on the site has a median answer time of 11 minutes [116].

Social coding sites GitHub and similar sites provide source code hosting with version control for software developers. However, these sites are also social network sites (cf. definition 8) and provide a high degree of social transparency [38]. Members are able to easily find out who they are interacting with, whom everyone else is interacting with, and who has interacted with which artifacts. This transparency influences the behavior of software developers [38]. For specific software engineering practices, the social transparency found on GitHub can have a large impact: Pham et al. [140] found that for testing, GitHub can help communicating requirements for tests and can prompt as well as motivate developers to provide tests with their contributions.

Developer profile aggregators   Using all the data that is available about an individual online, sites like Masterbranch and Coderwall create aggregate profiles for software developers. These sites use gamification [50] to motivate developers to try out new technologies and allow them to discover new contacts and technologies [162].

4.4. Summary

To support social processes, designers of collaboration systems attempt to model social cues. Awareness and social translucence are useful approaches for systems restricted to a certain number of users, but break down when social networks are used to structure applications — as is often the case in social media, for example. Social transparency is a theoretical framework for designing and analyzing such systems.

Many tools and services supporting social processes are already used in software engineering. The following chapter will first discuss challenges in the adoption of software engineering practices, and then show how support for social processes and other idiosyncrasies of groupware and social media systems can be used to address these challenges.

5. The Adoption of Software Engineering Practices

This chapter first shows that the adoption of software engineering practices is problematic, and that even mandating their use does not solve the problem. Instead, the introduction of obligatory practices can be met with resistance from developers.

The second part of this chapter reports on two studies I conducted on the use of social media by software developers. Together with colleagues, I found that social media provides several mechanisms that can support the diffusion and adoption of software engineering practices. This insight lays the groundwork for the contribution this thesis makes to improving adoption: using research results from social media, HCI, sociology, and psychology enables change agents to address practice adoption issues in a non-coercive manner, and can be achieved more systematically than currently practiced.

5.1. Adoption Problems

This section discusses practices in software engineering: their advantages, problems with their adoption, as well as consequences of and reasons for these adoption problems.

5.1.1. The Value of Software Engineering Practices

Software engineering practices, their supporting tools, and methodologies that prescribe more encompassing processes are used to improve the quality of software as well as the quality of the processes used to develop software. This can result in important competitive advantages for companies that are involved with creating software.

Several low-level practices have long been recommended in software engineering, for example using a version control system and writing readable code [77]. Even the concrete embodiments of these seemingly simple practices have been and still are subject to debate: the correct way to commit to git-based repositories is being debated on the Web[1]; Vermeulen et al. [188] give advice on how to write good code comments.

An example for a practice on a higher level of abstraction is test-driven development (TDD). Turhan et al. [181] note that, according to empirical studies, TDD can improve the quality of tests. Similarly, Tichy [179] shows that design patterns [69] improve development especially in maintenance. Employing design patterns can improve developers' productivity, reduce defects, and improve communication and knowledge diffusion between collaborating developers.

Other practices give advice on how developers should collaborate. For example, pair programming can lead to improvements in code correctness [192]. Cohen [29] notes that code reviews — in which other developers systematically examine one programmer's code for defects — are the fastest known practice for finding bugs.

Because of their positive influences on software quality, practices like TDD, design patterns, and code reviews can have a significant impact on the reliability, dependability, and security of software.

Yet more abstract than these team-oriented practices, processes and process improvement models give advice to whole organizations on how to structure their software development activities. In their systematic literature review on software process improvement (SPI) initiatives, Lavallée and Robillard [102] find that adopting mature development processes can reduce the significance of variations in developer capabilities. Without a formal process, the negative impact that developers of low proficiency could have on the final product would be much more severe than with such a process in place.

While researchers and practitioners do encounter disagreement and inconclusive evidence at times, empirical studies have shown that there *can be* concrete benefits to several software engineering practices.

5.1.2. Resistance to Practice Adoption

To achieve these benefits, practices have to be applied by developers. However, several studies show that organizations that try to introduce a practice or a whole methodology may encounter resistance from their employees [102, 174, 27, 84, 146, 61, 60]. The adoption of software engineering

---

[1]See, e.g., http://tbaggery.com/2008/04/19/a-note-about-git-commit-messages.html or http://sethrobertson.github.com/GitBestPractices/

practices, tools, and overarching methodologies has been the subject of scholarly debate for over 20 years [94].

- In their systematic literature review, Lavallée and Robillard [102] show that software process improvement initiatives that introduce new or modify existing practices are sometimes resisted by developers. As reasons for resistance, the authors for example report "a perceived increase in overhead", "fear that data collection will be used for personnel evaluation", and a perception of uselessness for certain practices.

- Hardgrave et al. [84] survey members of the IT department of a large company regarding their adoption of a methodology. They report that negative peer pressure can discourage developers from adopting.

- In a study of several companies of different sizes and from different industries, Fitzgerald [60] documents several incidents of methodologies that are "not followed rigorously" or whose implementation is "very patchy." For example, he describes how less experienced developers first follow a methodology and then become less formal in applying it once they have gained some experience. Fitzgerald finds that adherence to methodologies is negatively correlated with experience: experienced developers "know that they have to clean up the dirt later."

Any newly introduced practice will demand at least a certain change in behavior from developers, some even require drastic changes [27, 84]. Changing one's behavior, however, can be challenging — especially when the benefits are not immediate (cf. e.g. Rogers [149] on preventive innovations) or when the practice's usefulness is not visible for developers [102, 84, 146]. For some practices, their advantages might only be relevant for the organization, but not for the individual developers — e.g., those required for certifications or imposed by government policies [61]. As a consequence, organizations facing such resistance often cannot deploy their chosen practices or methodologies or at least not to full extent [84, 146].

5.1.3. Mandating Behavior

To counter resistance, organizations regularly *mandate* the application of certain practices and methodologies. Hardgrave et al. [84] studied the factors that determined whether developers would adopt a methodology. The authors find that mandating a behavior does indeed have an influence on adoption, but that several other factors can have an even greater influence. They conclude that an organizational mandate *"is not sufficient to guarantee use of the methodology in a sustained manner."* Riemenschneider et al. [146] arrive at a similar conclusion.

While mandatory adoption certainly helps in getting developers to adopt a practice, other determinants are still undervalued. Among these, the following were found to have the most impact.

- Perceived usefulness, perceived compatibility, and social pressure can have a stronger influence on developers than an organizational mandate [84, 146].

- Perceived developer involvement with and control over process changes as well as a transparent communication of such changes have a positive influence on adoption [182, 130, 139].

As Riemenschneider et al. [146] argue, alternative approaches that augment mandating behavior might alleviate adoption problems with software engineering practices and methodologies. The authors propose to use persuasive communication strategies to influence social pressure effects and developer motivation. As the rest of this chapter will show, social media and related technologies bear potential for supporting such a strategy.

5.1.4. Summary

This section has shown that while software engineering practices and methodologies are useful instruments to improve software products and the software development process, organizations can struggle with achieving sufficient adoption among their employees. Even though industry regularly mandates the adoption of practices, other factors are even more important — such as social pressure, perceived usefulness, and perceived compatibility. The remaining sections of this chapter present two empirical studies in which I, together with colleagues, investigated the use of social media by software developers and how they can influence these additional factors.

5.2. Empirical Study: Testing on GitHub

This section reports on an investigation of GitHub[2], the social coding site. Together with collaborators, I examined the influence of the social coding site's social transparency on the adoption and communication of software engineering practices — using testing as an example for such a practice [140]. Most of the developers we encountered work in organizations and engage in open source development either in their spare time or as part of their employment. As such, they are relevant subjects for investigating measures that could support the diffusion of software engineering practices in organizations.

Dabbish et al. [38] already explored whether and in which areas developers on GitHub are influenced by the site's peculiarities. One area in which they found effects was *software testing*. Our study investigates this in more depth. This report shows that even though developers in open source may also encounter practice adoption problems with their collaborators, social media can create useful effects and social dynamics to support practice adoption.

The next section introduces some necessary terminology used in Git and GitHub, after which our study is reported and discussed.

5.2.1. Terminology: Git and GitHub

Git[3] is a distributed version control system (DVCS). Each contributor may *clone* a remote repository to create a local copy of the whole repository and may then *commit* changes to this local repository. Changes can be *pushed* or *pulled* to and from remote repositories. Often, there is one remote repository combining the participants' commits.

To avoid having to grant every *contributor* full commit rights to that central repository, developers often use a process coined *forking*. Contributors create clones of the central repository and, eventually, if they want a commit to be included in the central repository, they issue a *pull request*: a notification to the *project owner* — the manager(s) of the central repository — that new commits are available on the developer's fork. The project owner may then decide themselves whether to pull those changes to the main repository. This decouples outside contributors from the central

---

[2]http://github.com
[3]http://git-scm.org

repository. For simplicity, we will refer to the project owner in the singular form, even though several developers might have that role for a project.

The social coding site GitHub[4] provides hosting of remote Git repositories and supports the repository interactions in a Web-based user interface. Pull requests can directly be commented on, thus facilitating discussions. GitHub integrates tools that are often used in software projects, such as an issue tracker or a wiki. Because of this easy accessibility and a streamlined contributing process, projects hosted on GitHub are accessible to a large number of potential collaborators.

Each member maintains a profile site, may *follow* the activities of other members, and may view the contact lists of other members — making GitHub a social network site as defined by Ellison and boyd [55]. Thus, project owners and contributing team members are easily reachable for potential external contributors.

5.2.2. Study Design

To explore how testing is carried out on social coding sites and how increased social transparency impacts the testing behavior of software developers engaged in those projects, we used an approach based on Grounded Theory (GT) [170]. For the purposes of our study, we focused on two groups of people: (1) *project owners* who receive pull requests and (2) *contributors* who send them.

Research Questions

We designed a set of research questions to better understand how testing practices evolve based on the interaction between contributors and project owners on social coding sites. First, we focused on identifying the main steps and variations of the contribution process and how decisions are made with regard to testing. This leads to our first research question:

RQ1: What is the contribution process with regard to testing on social coding sites?

While investigating the contribution process on GitHub, it became clear that contributions were assessed by project owners. Furthermore, we found different motivations for implementing quality assurance measures specific to interaction on social coding sites. We refined our first research question into two subquestions to accommodate this.

---

[4]http://github.com

RQ1.1: How do project owners assess incoming contributions from contributors?

RQ1.2: What are the internal and external motivations for engaging in testing efforts on social coding sites?

As reported by Stuart et al. [171], social transparency may have hard to anticipate second order effects in addition to the possibly intended first order effects. In our study, we wanted to find out more about the issues that might arise as a result of those effects. As such, our second research question is:

RQ2: What challenges and risks related to testing arise from engaging in projects on social coding sites?

In face of such challenges and risks, project owners and contributors might have to evolve and adapt their contribution process. For example, project owners might have to advise contributors on how to conform to project guidelines. Our third research question focuses on the actions taken by each group of actors for overcoming such issues:

RQ3: How do developers cope with those challenges and risks?

Finally, the increased social transparency on social coding sites creates distinct modes of interaction between project collaborators. Understanding these modes of interaction can help guiding approaches that attempt to improve the adoption of testing practices, such as the one presented in this thesis. This leads to our last research question:

RQ4: What impact does the participation on social coding projects have on testing practices?

Procedure

Grounded Theory [170] emphasizes a continuous data collection process interlaced with periodic pauses for analysis. As such, we conducted our study in three phases.

First, we focused on understanding which testing-related norms and conventions exist on GitHub. For our investigation, we obtained 16,000 email addresses of recently active users by querying the GitHub Archive[5]. From this pool, we invited 50 users to semi-structured interviews, and another 50 users by randomly choosing a member from each of the 50 most successful GitHub teams as listed on the Coderwall[6] leaderboard. This sampling

---

[5]http://www.githubarchive.org
[6]http://coderwall.com

strategy resulted in a diverse population: highly experienced as well as regular users of GitHub.

Of these 100 users, 10 from the former sample and 3 from the latter sample enrolled. Each participant was interviewed by a member of our research team via voice call. Interviews lasted approximately 20 minutes and the audio was recorded. We asked the participants to outline the testing process in one of their public projects on GitHub. Preliminary findings indicated that projects featuring extensive collaboration between developers would demand more elaborate testing approaches. We also learned that most decisions regarding testing were made when pull requests were sent and received, i.e., when people had to coordinate and negotiate their cooperation.

In the second phase of our research, we defined our target population to be active users who used the collaboration features of GitHub. From our address pool, we invited 1,000 GitHub users at random to take our first questionnaire: 500 at first and again 500 after 6 days. In total, 158 users responded, of which 74 left usable contact information. The questionnaire responses allowed us to distinguish between users that had been collaboratively active — they had either sent a pull request or forked a project — and their approaches for testing contributions. We invited all 62 of those 74 who matched our criteria for another round of semi-structured interviews. 20 users enrolled.

In these interviews, we inquired about participants' testing practices and values. We had prior answers to these questions from the questionnaire and used the interviews to explore such situations in detail, allowing us to better understand the contribution process with a focus on testing behavior and practices. For example, we asked interviewees how they *handled incoming pull requests* and whether they had any kind of quality assurance measures related to this process. Then, we inquired about their motivations for assuring quality and the challenges they face when *contributing* to other projects. As a result of our second phase, we were able to identify five themes that stood out.

1. The fork and pull request mechanisms, social network features, and integration of numerous tools result in a *GitHub-specific process* for sending and receiving contributions.

2. GitHub makes it easier to access a public repository, start working on it, handle contributions, and discuss them with contributors. GitHub

tools and social features *lower the barriers for engagement* in software projects.

3. Public projects and profiles on GitHub have *high exposure* to many potential contributors and users. This helps with, for example, discovering edge cases.

4. GitHub *integrates* many tools into the project context and *centralizes* many interactions and notifications among project participants.

5. GitHub provides increased *social transparency* that allows its users to see the identity, actions, and communications between users, a phenomenon that was previously reported on by Dabbish et al. [38].

In the last phase, a final questionnaire was sent to 4,000 random GitHub users for a quantitative validation of our findings. Of these users, 569 responded. The results of this phase can be found in section 5.2.4.

Data Analysis

We alternated periods of data collection with analysis in order to build up our theory. At the end of each data collection phase, we transcribed the recorded interviews and open coded them. This resulted in 172 codes that we consolidated to 45 codes through discussions among all authors. At the end of our second phase, we engaged in axial coding in order to find higher level conceptual themes that would help us in answering our research questions[7]. In the last phase of our research, core themes of our theory were formed into statements and validated through a final questionnaire (cf. section 5.2.4). Participants were asked to agree or disagree with statements using a Likert scale. For each question, the mean value for the given set of answers was calculated, as well as its variance and the number of given answers to that question in total. For questions that required the participant to choose an answer in a set of pre-given answers, the count for each answer was calculated and related to the total number of answers to that question.

Participants

Overall, we interviewed 33 people, among them software developers, testers, and software architects. Nearly half of them were using GitHub for pro-

---

[7]The coding system can be found in appendix A.

fessional work (19); the other half (14) used GitHub for private projects. Our population comprised of developers employed in a software company (24), self-employed (3), and unemployed developers (2). 4 interviewees were affiliated with universities and mostly engaged in noncommercial projects.

20 participants of our second interview phase estimated the number of total contributors to their projects. Numbers of contributors were diverse: 12 projects with up to ten contributors, two projects with up to one hundred contributors and six projects with over one hundred contributors. We denote these interviewees from the second phase with *FI*. Randomly chosen interviewees from the first interview round are denoted with *R*, Coderwall leaderboard members are denoted with *L*.

5.2.3. Findings

Interaction on GitHub With Regard to Testing

This section reports on our findings regarding the contribution process on GitHub and how project owners assess pull requests from contributors (RQ 1.1).

In the course of our interviews, several steps of the contribution process on GitHub emerged. After receiving a pull request, the first step that project owners conducted was to manually review the contribution and assess it by different aspects. After this review, they merged the pull request into a testing branch and resolved conflicts manually. Superficial adjustments like code style corrections or comments were added based on preference. If a test suite existed, project owners ran it to check whether or not this contribution passed tests. This heightened confidence in the contribution. Finally, the contribution was merged into the main branch of the project.

We found many factors that were taken into consideration by project owners when assessing contributions. For instance, project owners reported to treat incoming pull requests differently depending on whether they **trusted** the contributing developer. Pull requests from unknown developers would undergo a more thorough assessment, while contributions from trusted developers would be merged right away. *"if it's someone I trust, who's worked on the project a lot, then I don't do that. [...] if it's someone who hasn't spent a lot of time on the project, I'll try and do that." [L48]*

The perceived **size of the changes** highly influenced the project owner's need for tests. If the project owner believed to have quickly understood the changes' impact, they demanded no tests from the contributor. This was often the case when only some lines of code had been changed.

Additionally, project owners distinguished between two **types of contributions**: contributions that introduced a new feature or contributions that changed existing code, such as bug fixes. The former were requested to include tests, while the latter caused project owners to check whether or not the changed code was already covered by existing tests. If so, no further tests were demanded. *"if you really write a new feature, then it makes more sense to add tests for that, but if you just do a little change in a code chunk that is already there then I don't expect that the person writes the test for that." [FI19]*

The **target of the changes** was considered as well. Changes to core functionality caused a demand for tests. However, if the **estimated effort** for creating automated tests was regarded as infeasible, this demand was waived. Often, such tests would require a cumbersome setup of test environments (such as different operating systems). Project owners were aware that contributors acted voluntarily and were unfunded in most cases.

Motivations for Demanding and Delivering Tests

This section presents our findings regarding project owners' motivations for demanding tests and contributors' motivations for providing them (RQ 1.2).

Project owners' reasons for demanding tested contributions were manifold. Maintaining clean and well documented code reduced the subsequent **support effort**, according to one project owner. Some project owners perceived tests as a form of **documentation** of how to use the contributed feature. Another project owner requested contributors to provide test cases of how they needed the software to behave, so he could merge these into the existing test suite for future regression testing. In this case, tests were used for **communicating requirements**.

An external motivator was the impression of acting as a **role model** when working on a testing-related project. Several users reported to feel obliged to perform proper quality assurance for projects with a **domain related to testing** — e.g. a testing framework or a continuous integration server.

In interviews with contributors, different motivations for including tests in pull request on one's own initiative emerged. Some interviewees said they explicitly added tests that **highlight the value** of their contribution to the project owner: these tests failed with the old version of the software in question, but passed when the contribution was applied.

The *existence and prominent placement of tests* gave contributors the impression of informal project guidelines; thus they felt obligated to add their own tests. *"[There were no guidelines set up], not so much formally, but it was pretty clear how it was supposed to be tested and there was already an existing spec file [...] with a pretty substantial list of tests"* [FI17]

Similar to a project owner perceiving oneself as a role model when working on a testing-related project, contributors felt an *implicit demand* for tested pull requests in such projects. In other instances, this obligation also resulted from customs rooted in the community of the technology used. Often, Ruby developers tested their contribution by default.

Challenges and Risks

This section discusses the challenges and risks we found to arise when engaging with projects on GitHub (RQ 2).

Interviewees saw an *urgent need for automatic tests* in their projects. This need was felt very strongly, as there are a lot of contributors on GitHub which are often only marginally engaged, i.e., there is a large group of developers in the periphery. Therefore, a lot of contributions need to be managed which interviewees reported could not be done using manual tests — simply for *reasons of scale*. *"a lot of people are contributing to [the project] and quality control is becoming more and more important to us. Automated testing is the only way to get that"* [FI7] To achieve automated testing, project owners were in many cases looking for tests when they received pull requests from contributors (cf. the previous section).

Because there is a *constant flux of contributors*, and developers new to a project are not yet accustomed to its testing culture, they have to learn it anew. This takes time and effort. If a project fails to *communicate testing culture* efficiently and effectively, or sets *barriers that are too high* for first-time contributors, it can struggle to create such a culture. For example, if new contributors cannot easily find *existing tests* in a project, they will not be able to write any of their own for their contributions. *"When I first started contributing to [the project], they did not actually have a test suite which made shipping them tests fairly difficult"* [FI20]

Several project owners reported that their projects were *struggling with creating the required testing culture*. The pull requests they received would often not include any tests by default. One issue they saw was the **voluntary nature of open source** contributions: they could not simply require well-tested contributions. Developers who had sent a valuable pull request might be alienated if project owners rejected their contributions due to a lack of tests. *"We have a project, where we don't have the culture, it is difficult and people are volunteers, we can't just enforce it on the project. You have to try to incubate it into the project."* [FI7]

Another reason why creating a robust testing culture is so difficult could be the lack of experience on the side of the contributors. As one developer from a commercial project said, *"We have a lot of people ramping up to the team every time. So, we have a big rotation. So new people don't understand what is a quick build, what is the regression, what is isolated, ... and they don't understand how to write tests for each of those suites."* [L4]

Two of GitHub's greatest strengths — low barriers to contribution, combined with tight integration of related tools and services — are related to another challenge that interviewees mentioned. In terms of testing, there are **no integrated tools** provided by GitHub that might lower some testing-related barriers, e.g. for setting up a server for continuous integration. Even though this is starting to be supported by Travis CI[8], this was not yet commonly used among the interviewed population. One interviewee even mentioned that *"github its such an easy-to-use-tool that it makes writing unit tests seem like extra time for most people."* [R16]

Coping with Challenges

In this section, we report how interviewees coped with the testing-related challenges on GitHub (RQ 3).

As described in the previous section, scalability reasons drive project owners towards automated tests. However, manually merging each pull request into a testing branch and running regression tests with a test suite of automated tests remained a tedious task. Some interviewees resorted to an **automated continuous integration** (CI) service, such as Travis CI or Jenkins. Such a service frees the project owner of several manual steps: when a pull requests is received, a program merges the contribution into a testing branch, runs the existing test suite, and notifies the project owner as well as the contributor of the results.

---

[8]http://travis-ci.org

Project owners developed different strategies to establish a common understanding of testing requirements and handling untested pull requests. Due to the voluntary nature of GitHub (c.f. previous section), some project owners simply resorted to **writing tests themselves** or **thankfully requesting** — instead of demanding — further tests, as this leaves the contributor the option to decline.

Lowering the barriers and making it **easier to provide tests** was another strategy, for example by introducing a testing framework with a suitable explanation of its usage. Other project owners provided **easy access to learning resources** and **actively supported** contributors who showed difficulties in writing tests: pointing contributors to tutorials, suitable examples in an existing test suite, or actively teaching them. This was beneficial as contributors were convinced of the need for tests and included tests on their own in subsequent pull requests. *"[...] I can point them to one of the existing tests. «Check this one, it is really similar to what you need», and in most cases it's enough. Sometimes, [...] I do Skype conferences with screen sharing where I can explain, show." [FI4]*

A passive strategy for communication testing requirements was to make it more **obvious** that testing was indeed desired by giving the impression that testing was customary in one's project. Some interviewees said that they tried to **lead by example** and tried to make testing visible in the project, hoping to engage contributors in testing. Another strategy was to **display testing signals**. For example, every project using Travis CI may add a badge to its profile page (cf. Fig. 5.1). This informs a potential contributor that continuous integration is regularly performed. *"if you see that image, it immediately rings the bell that there is continuous integration in this project, and as such, there is some kind of automated testing." [FI6]*

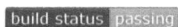

Figure 5.1: *The Travis CI badge that projects may add to their GitHub profile page, signifying the status of the last build.*

Impact of Social Coding Sites on Testing Practices

This section investigates the impact of engaging with a social coding site on testing practices (RQ 4).

During our research, we encountered different levels of lowering the effort for testing. One interviewee suggested that in his perception, projects using BDD and concentrating on testing primarily the *main use cases* provided these low barriers to entry. This allowed those projects to deliver results very fast, which impressed other developers. Those projects were also very good at communicating their culture in social media, e.g. via blog posts advocating their testing culture. This combination, the interviewee said, would lead to the described behavior being adopted at a fast rate and thus spreading through GitHub. He saw this development critically however, as possibly important edge cases were ignored until they became apparent.

A more extreme case of lowering the barrier for contributions was simply to *defer testing* to a later stage of the project. An interviewee said that in his experience, younger projects needed to gain traction in the present. Obtaining external contributions was regarded to be more important than quality assurance measures. However, such projects would need to pay back this accumulated technical debt in the future.

Interviewees told us that effectively *communicating a project's testing culture* would lead to contributors adopting that culture more rapidly and in greater numbers. We spoke to several developers who had experiences in multiple projects with different communication strategies. According to them, better communication of testing culture leads to more pull requests containing tests, and therefore to projects that were tested better. *Testing guidelines* and *actively communicating* to contributors what kind of tests were required helped getting more contributors to provide tests with their pull requests. Providing guidelines on contributing or dedicated testing tutorials was reported to remove uncertainties in contributors about how to participate correctly. This way, the barrier of having to ask was removed. One interviewee expressed that knowing a project's testing culture and adhering to it would make him and his peers feel *proud*, further helping the project's testing culture to be adopted. However, the reverse was also mentioned: if a project did not communicate anything about its norms and requirements regarding testing, new contributors would simply *assume that no tests had to be written* and consequently submit pull requests not containing any.

Some interviewees mentioned that testing culture — and communicating it — could even be ingrained not only in a single project, but in a whole *infrastructure community* (c.f. section 5.2.3). According to these interviewees, in the Ruby community it was taken for granted that blog posts, screencasts, and tweets from popular developers often talked about testing practices that were regarded as proper in that community. This is a form of communicating a testing culture — in this case however, in a much larger realm than that of one or more GitHub projects.

Interviewees reported several examples where **direct exchanges** on GitHub helped diffusing testing culture. For example, one project owner reported that his project started using the Travis CI service when it received a pull request that added a Travis CI configuration file. *"I received a Travis CI config [in a pull request]. I did not know this service before and someone send me a config for Travis and this is how I came to use it" [FI19]*

Travis CI, in turn, also arranges for **low barriers** and **easy communication** of testing culture. As described in section 5.2.3, the Travis CI badge is perceived as a signal that communicates the use of certain practices.

However, employing a continuous integration service with an extensive test suite may create a **false sense of security**: one interviewee reported to use the positive result of running his existing test suite as a sufficient confirmation of a contribution's correctness. He usually simply merged such pull requests without requesting any additional tests specific to these contributions.

A key instrument for project owners wishing to create and nurture their project's testing culture was to provide existing tests and a testing infrastructure that was easy to set up (c.f. section 5.2.3). Interviewees reported this to **lower the barrier** to accommodate to the project's culture. They would just need to fork the project, execute a shell command, and have the existing tests running. Interviewees took this as an opportunity to run regression tests, thus trying to make sure that their contribution did not break anything. This heightened their confidence in the correctness of their own code and lowered the barrier of contributing. Some interviewees also said that just having a test suite would **communicate certain values** regarding testing, helping them understand the project's testing culture, norms, and conventions. Providing **publicly available tests** brought by another advantage: contributors heavily used existing tests as a source for education and examples for their own test cases. *"there were some tests surrounding some quite similar functionality in the source, so I basically copied and modified these tests to test the functionality that I added." [FI20]*

One recurring theme was that a better communication of testing culture and low barriers in a project *promote exploration and experimentation* for new contributors. Interviewees claimed that this, in turn, often leads to developers becoming more familiar with a project's testing culture, making it easier for them to provide their own tests. For example, a project with a CI server that provided fast feedback on tests was said to support experimentation — after all, problems would be easily visible, giving experimenting developers more confidence. Some interviewees mentioned that experimentation was supported not only by a project's deliberate efforts, but also by the chosen programming language and the available libraries.

Interviewees claimed that the number of volunteer contributions increased since moving their projects to GitHub. They attributed this to the low barriers to entry and the resulting exposure to a larger number of developers. An employee of a company that develops open and closed source projects told us that many GitHub contributors find bugs, provide tests, and send them bug fixes. This, he claimed, enabled the company's paid developers to *concentrate on larger issues*, such as creating new features.

To a greater extent, interviewees reported that the *public nature* of software development on GitHub leads to an improvement of testing practices. Some of them were companies that used the exemplary testing practices in their public projects as an *advertisement* for the high quality of their development services. Indeed, one employee of such a company confided that testing was less important in the company's internal projects, as they did not serve as such advertisements.

We heard similar reports from open source projects not backed by companies. Core members of such projects were concerned about the project's *reputation* — how the project was perceived by the community. They believed that proper testing would lead to higher quality code, which in turn would be received better by others. *"we need to have a more substantial testing framework because it's [...] a significant indicator of code quality in the community. If you don't have good tests then people start to suspect that your code may not be any good either."* [FI17]

On the side of the contributors, one interviewee reported that having contributed to a high-profile project in which tests are mandatory would help him *find work*. Indeed, that was his only reason for contributing.

Our findings show that several mechanisms and processes used on GitHub may help projects become better tested. Project owners help new contributors get acquainted with a project's culture and make it easy for them to get up and running technically. However, this does not only affect regular contributors that can be productive faster. ***Drive-by commits*** — as an interviewee called them — are small changes that do not require a prolonged engagement with a project, yet provide some value for it. Developers providing such changes would not always be actively interested in a project, but might have stumbled upon it when browsing GitHub. Then, when they had found, for example, a spelling error or a missing translation, they would make a quick correction and forget the project again. This might lead to GitHub having a very long tail of very many very small contributions.

5.2.4. Validation of our Findings

In the previous section, we presented findings gathered by conducting interviews with 33 users of GitHub. This section presents the most striking results of our final questionnaire that we used to validate core statements of our findings. Of 4,000 random GitHub users, 569 completed this questionnaire. Our results are summarized in Table 5.1. *PO* denotes statements about project owners, *C* about contributors. For each question, we presented the participant with a Likert scale: the value of 1 represents "I do not agree at all" and 5 means "I strongly agree."

The questionnaire required the participant to take both the perspective of a project owner and a contributor. 39% of our participants would receive pull requests at least a few times per week (daily: 16%) and 27% send pull requests at least a few times per week (daily: 6%).

Even though several interviewees mentioned voluntarism as a hindering factor, the questionnaire did not validate this (PO1). Personal traits such as modesty and humility of the requester as well as value given to the contribution may be influencing factors.

Similarly, most of the participants did not agree to feel a need for automation (PO2). However, as some interviewees mentioned, this need may depend on the size and popularity of the project in question. As popularity grows, the amount of incoming pull requests increases. As both samples were randomly invited, but ultimately self-selected, variations in populations might attribute for this dissonance.

Interpreting results to statements PO3 and PO4 in conjunction to statements C2, C3, and C4 creates an interesting image. Project owners agree that providing tests in one's project lowers the support effort regarding

Statement	Question	Results
PO1:Voluntarism hinders demand of tests.	I have the feeling that I am not in position to demand tests from a contributor as he or she is contributing on a voluntary basis.	A: 2,21 V: 1,44 N: 464
PO2: Amount of incoming pull requests demands for automation.	The amount of incoming pull requests is so big that I can only assure their quality by using automated tests.	A: 2,32 V: 1,57 N: 453
PO3: Existing tests support contributors in writing their own tests.	When I have tests in my project, contributors need less help in writing tests.	A: 4,09 V: 0,91 N: 457
PO4: Existing tests facilitate more incoming pull requests that are tested.	As a consequence of providing tests in my project, more pull requests include tests.	A: 3,64 V: 1,12 N: 452
C1: Low barrier commit mechanism facilitates Drive-By-Commits.	Since it is so easy to send a pull request, I contribute more changes that I would not have engaged in otherwise.	A: 3,98 V: 1,33 N: 496
C2: Existing tests make contributor feel obligated to add tests.	When I see that there are tests in a project, I will also include tests in my pull request.	A: 4,09 V: 1,06 N: 499
C3: Existing tests are a source of education for contributors.	Existing tests help me in understanding how to test in a specific project.	A: 4,52 V: 0,61 N: 495
C4: Contributors use existing tests as a basis for new tests.	I use existing tests as a basis for my own tests: I copy and paste them and adjust them accordingly.	A: 3,94 V: 1,06 N: 496

Table 5.1.: *Questionnaire results. A: average value; V: variance; N: number of answers.*

testing by contributors (PO3). Appropriately, contributors heavily rely on existing test cases when creating their own. They use these to learn how testing is done in a specific project (C3) and, lastly, even copy existing tests and use them as a basis for new tests (C4).

With tests in place, contributors feel obligated to add their own tests and seem to comply with this implicit demand (C2). Yet, project owners do not seem to see a meaningful relation between providing tests and the amount of incoming pull requests that include tests (PO4). Project owners possibly overlook this connection between the existence of a publicly accessible test suite and the test behavior of contributors. For further insights on this, however, more in-depth research is needed.

5.2.5. Discussion

This section relates our work to previous research and discusses its potential impact on the software development industry, open source development, and research. We connect our findings with research in Communities of Practice and the diffusion of innovations. In doing so, we distinguish between processes occurring inside of projects — intra-project — and those spanning multiple projects, i.e., inter-project processes.

Creating a Shared Understanding

Lave and Wenger [103] coined the term *Community of Practice* (CoP) for groups of individuals that work on similar problems and exchange knowledge about good practices and proven solutions with each other. They mention *legitimate peripheral participation* as a central phenomenon when describing how new members of the CoP join and, through learning the community's norms, become more and more involved with it. Initially, novices merely observe practices passively before starting to take on simple and increasingly complex tasks. New members are said to be situated in the community's periphery, while established members are part of the core. As shown by Crowston et al. [34], these processes can apply to open source software development as well.

Intra-project Processes Inside of individual projects, we found that new contributors start off with first observing how pull requests are handled and discussed, and what good commits and tests look like. This is supported by the high social transparency found on GitHub.

When they are ready to submit their own pull requests, they have already learned quite a lot about the project's testing culture. However, they are often assisted further by the low barriers many projects on GitHub strive to provide to potential contributors. Examples for this are existing tests that can be simply copied and modified, as well as the fact that several project owners told us that they strive to provide testing infrastructure that is easy to set up. This is again supported by test automation integrated with GitHub itself, such as Travis CI.

This increased level of support for peripheral contributors seemingly creates very large peripheries of contributors for projects, as touched upon in some of our interviews. Consequently, some of the mechanisms we found may be used solely for managing peripheries of this greater size. Because of the exploratory nature of this work, we were not yet able to gain deeper insights about the properties of such projects. Future research will need to investigate the problems created by projects with such compositions and how project members manage these challenges.

Drive-by commits — simple commits that leave their creators rather uninvolved with the project and that can be created with very little project-specific knowledge — are a departure from the model of the peripheral member that gradually gets more involved with a community. We believe that more research is needed to help us understand the motivations and processes surrounding this phenomenon better.

Inter-project Processes   In addition to these phenomenons related to individual projects, some interviewees told us about how testing culture functions for communities that span multiple disconnected projects. Most of the time, these would use the same programming language and the same frameworks for development.

For example, the Ruby community seems to have a distinguished testing culture that many interviewees were aware of. Core members of the community create the frameworks that more peripheral members will use, and also publish learning resources such as blog posts and screencasts. In these frameworks and documents, they advocate a certain testing culture: e.g., behavior-driven development (BDD), supported by BDD testing frameworks, and characterized by a focus on testing primarily the *happy path* — the intended behavior, ignoring edge cases for a large part.

As one interviewer opined, frameworks and the respective testing culture allow such projects to move very fast and to produce impressive results more easily. He argued that this was part of why the testing culture gets easily adopted by novice community members.

Diffusion of Testing Practices

GitHub does not only help Communities of Practice create a shared understanding of their respective testing culture in peripheral and novice contributors. It also facilitates the diffusion of these practices among developers inside and outside of individual communities.

Research on the diffusion of innovations investigates how and why tools, practices, ideas, or technologies perceived as new — *innovations* — are adopted by individuals and groups. Rogers [149] documents properties of innovations that were discovered to support their adoption across many different scenarios (cf. chapter 2).

- *Relative Advantage:* adoption is more likely if the innovation has a clear advantage with regard to known alternatives.

- *Compatibility:* the more compatible an innovation is to a person's existing practices, the more likely it is that she will adopt it.

- *Complexity:* the more complex an innovation is perceived to be, the less likely it will be adopted.

- *Observability:* an innovation will be more likely to be adopted the easier it is to observe existing adopters.

- *Trialability:* the easier it is to try out an innovation before deciding to adopt it, the more likely it is to be adopted.

We now relate these properties to the phenomenons we found in our work.

Intra-project Processes   Positive results of testing practices, such as adding features fast or badges with passing test results, demonstrate the *relative advantage* of those practices. As project owners strive to make it easy for new contributors to get started with their project and its test suite, they actively improve their project's *technical compatibility* with developers' existing practices. In the same vein, by communicating desired testing behavior and aligning it with the values promoted by thought leaders, they improve their project's *cultural compatibility*. By lowering the barriers to entry — e.g., by providing existing tests, examples, and a working infrastructure for automated tests — project owners reduce the perceived *complexity* of their project's testing practices. Several integration and user interface features of GitHub support his, such as the built-in ticket system, external services like Travis CI, or the comfort with which code can be inspected using a Web browser.

Low barriers also increase the *trialability* of testing practices. If developers want to try a project out themselves, all they have to do is clone the repository to their local machine using a single command. For certain communities, one more command will install all dependencies and run the project's tests: one interviewee noted how the Ruby community makes this process especially easy.

Finally, the social transparency on GitHub makes testing practices more *observable*. By looking at commits, issues, pull requests, and the respective discussions surrounding those items, developers on GitHub are able to observe the testing culture in a project without needing to become involved much.

Inter-project Processes   As reported by several interviewees, they also use GitHub to discover new projects, and to learn more about those they already know about. Being able to follow the activity of developers and to browse projects by technological niche support this discovery. In this regard, the aforementioned properties of GitHub apply not only to individual projects, but also to the diffusion of testing practices *across* projects. For example, one interviewee told us that he uses GitHub to learn how other projects use the testing framework that his work project uses (L4). This shows how these mechanisms are even able to diffuse practices into organizations not necessarily hosting their projects on GitHub (which was the case for L4).

Impact

We discovered several mechanisms that help creating a shared understanding of a project's testing culture and diffuse testing practices to other individuals and groups. Because of the exploratory nature of our research, we have not yet discovered best practices, but candidates for such. From these mechanisms, we can derive several preliminary guidelines.

Companies and core members of software projects should strive to *lower the barriers* to testing by providing testing guidelines, test examples, an easy to set up testing infrastructure, and integrated automatic testing. Doing so should support cultivating a project culture that embraces appropriate testing practices, ideally leading to higher quality software products. Project participants learning these practices will be able to apply their testing knowledge in future projects, which would be especially helpful in diffusing these practices in organizations.

Projects should visibly communicate their testing culture by providing a high degree of social transparency. Showing that the normative behavior in a project is to provide certain kinds of tests should help developers adopt these practices more easily. Testing culture can be picked up by new developers if they can observe the discussions surrounding changes, making it easier to understand the requirements of a project and the rationales behind them. This may be supported by clearly communicating what the testing status of a project is, e.g. by displaying a badge or by providing a more detailed project dashboard.

These results suggest concrete strategies that could be used to improve the adoption of not only testing practices, but software engineering practices in general. As such, some of the adoption patterns (cf. chapter 7) reference some results of this study.

5.2.6. Limitations

Our study is a first, exploratory investigation into the effects that the characteristics of social coding sites like GitHub may have on testing practices. Therefore, we chose an approach based on Grounded Theory. While we achieved saturation in our interviews, it is likely that we did not reach all possible perspectives on GitHub use. Even though we sent out interview invitations to active but random users of GitHub, the final interview participants were all self-selected volunteers.

Similarly, the participants of our questionnaire were again chosen randomly, but ultimately were self-selected. The quantitative validation of our results therefore is again only applicable to the volunteering sub-population. The general population of GitHub might have different characteristics and opinions.

Apart from the questionnaire, we cannot provide quantifiable results. We cannot judge the strength or pervasiveness of any of the presented processes, mechanisms, or effects.

Finally, our results are not generalizable. We provide a view of testing on GitHub as seen by a certain self-selected population.

Yet, our research identified current challenges and solutions that are used in commercial and hobbyist open source software development. These are good indicators for the applicability of social media mechanisms such as social transparency to the problem of practice adoption addressed by this thesis.

5.2.7. Conclusions

When hosting a project on a social coding site such as GitHub, project owners interact with external contributors with varying knowledge and values regarding testing. Communicating a project's testing culture to such a population is an important, yet difficult task. In commercial software development projects, similar communication is required, e.g. to introduce new employees to a project.

In our study, we found how social transparency supports developers on GitHub in communicating and diffusing the testing practices they have chosen for their projects. While several project owners reported adoption issues, others told us about possible solutions: clearly communicating testing requirements to achieve better adoption; awareness features to support the formation of normative behavior; and examples that are easily customizable lower barriers for newcomers.

Even though projects on GitHub can struggle with the adoption of testing practices by contributors, we found that social media can support the adoption process. Using these effects systematically may thus be a viable strategy to improve the adoption of software engineering practices in organizations.

Differences between public open source development and private commercial development in organizations should have an influence on the applicability of social media effects in these different scenarios. However, similarities can also be expected and uncovered by relating our findings to theories on human behavior that are also relevant in organizations. For example, communities of practice exist in companies as well, and Rogers' diffusion of innovations model is also applicable to such organizations.

The following section reports on another study, in which we investigated a category of social media for developers that are further away from the development process than GitHub: *developer profile aggregators*.

5.3. Empirical Study: Mutual Assessment in Social Media for Developers

The previous section investigated the influence of GitHub on developers' behaviors. Yet, developers use social media to a much larger extent — GitHub is only a single site in a larger ecosystem. To access this ecosystem and to investigate which consequences participation in the ecosystem has for developers, this section reports on a study of *developer profile aggregators* [162] — Masterbranch[9] and Coderwall[10].

Masterbranch and Coderwall are examples of websites specifically created for the self-display of software developers, aggregating data from other sites such as GitHub and Stack Overflow[11]. As our study finds, these sites provide access to a community of innovative software developers who are active in open source development and are either working in companies or as contractors. As such, they are suitable study subjects for exploring the influence of social media on software engineers.

Developers' participation on these sites influences how they manage their reputation and how others engage with them. Developers use social media to connect with their communities and to monitor, publicize, and grow their skill sets. Social media are connecting like-minded developers, resulting in new social ties that foster collaboration and can encourage entrepreneurship at international scale. By using Masterbranch and Coderwall as an entry point, we survey and interview participants of the *social programmer ecosystem*. Our approach allows us to find the motivations and strategies for participating in this ecosystem.

We use the following terminology. A *profile* is a webpage that contains information about a user of the associated website. Profiles play a part in managing one's *public image*, that is, the way one is perceived publicly. *Social network sites* allow their users to create a profile, to connect with each other, and to inspect each other's connections with other users of the site [20] — examples are LinkedIn, Twitter, and GitHub. Masterbranch and Coderwall are *developer profile aggregators*, as they create profiles out of several existing profiles and activities on other sites for a single user.

---

[9]http://masterbranch.com
[10]http://coderwall.com
[11]https://masterbranch.com/html/about.html

5.3.1. Background

This section discusses research on profiles in online communities and their influences on human behavior. Following this, we introduce the two websites that we investigated as our window into the social programmer ecosystem.

Profiles in Online Communities

The importance of public user profiles for online communities and how people choose to manage their profiles in those communities is well established. One of the most extensively studied social media communities is Wikipedia [106, 96, 142, 74]. Since its inception in 2001, the online encyclopedia has become a reference model for how an online community can organize, collaborate, share, and create. Online communities such as Wikipedia are open collaborative spaces that allow virtually anybody to contribute. Because of this inherent openness, the quality, accountability, and trustworthiness of contributions is often suspect. Therefore, it is important that a community be able to quickly and adequately evaluate a user's contributions to that community.

Several authors have discussed the issue of trust in online communities and how trust issues can be mitigated through the application of theories of social translucence and social transparency [56, 171, 172] (cf. chapter 4). In online communities, different levels of transparency cause different behaviors. As discussed in the previous chapter, higher identity transparency increases actor accountability: members are more likely to act in an accountable manner if their profile is available for other community members to review. Also, members can better assess the quality of information based on reputational accountability of the source. This effect has been shown by Hess and Stein in a study on Wikipedia's "featured articles" (articles voted by the community to be of very high quality) [167]. They found that articles with contributions from higher reputation authors — as judged from their public profiles — were more likely to become featured articles. However, a negative consequence of higher identity transparency could be that creativity suffers due to members not wishing to contribute information that, while potentially valuable to the community, might negatively affect their reputation.

Dabbish et al. investigate how software developers manage their online profiles by studying GitHub users [38]. They find that while explicit self-promotion is frowned upon, users are actively managing their public image and that users believe visibility to be important for the success of an open source project. Watching and being watched also have benefits and requirements. Users say that having watchers is a motivation to continue making contributions. Also, they are more conscious of the quality of their contributions when a project has more watchers.

Developer Profile Aggregators

A recent trend in social media for software development is the emergence of profile aggregation sites for developers, such as Masterbranch and Coderwall. These websites are specifically tailored to software developers and aggregate developers' activities from across several other websites, providing a combined social programmer meta-profile. Contrary to more established sites, such as ohloh[12], Masterbranch and Coderwall focus on the developer rather than on individual projects.

Both sites provide public developer profiles that are mostly generated from activities on social code sharing sites such as GitHub, BitBucket[13], or SourceForge[14]. Other sites, such as LinkedIn[15] and Stack Overflow, are also supported. The customers of both sites are companies that are looking to hire software developers, for which the sites provide them with special access to their databases of developer profiles. According to their operators, Masterbranch and Coderwall both aim to make it easier for their customers to find candidates suitable for hiring. Customers of Masterbranch so far are mainly web-focused companies of all sizes, most of them younger than 10 years, and some of them very well-known.

Masterbranch

Masterbranch was founded in 2009 by Ignacio Andreu, Juan Luis Belmonte, and Vanessa Ramos. In 2011, the creators started growing it into a community for software developers. As of February 20th 2012, more than 9,000 users had registered with the site.

Fig. 5.2 shows a screenshot of a developer profile[16]. On top, it displays the name, location, and image of the user, as well as the *DevScore* (a value

---

[12]http://ohloh.net
[13]http://bitbucket.org/
[14]http://sourceforge.net/
[15]http://linkedin.com
[16]Taken from http://masterbranch.com/lsinger

calculated from the developer's activities, such as commits to projects). To the right, a button allows users to *give free beer* to the developer — a symbolic act of endorsement.

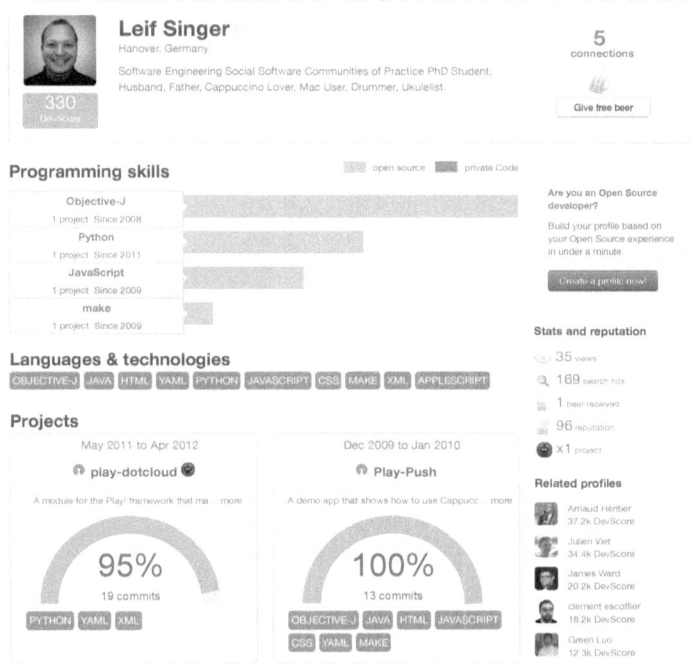

Figure 5.2: *A developer profile on Masterbranch.*

A table generated from the user's repositories displays the distribution of programming languages across these projects. Next, the profile lists projects the developer has worked on. For each project, the name, duration, description, and the programming languages used are displayed. The blue arcs indicate the percentage of commits the user contributed to a project.

Masterbranch awards *Most Valuable Programmer* (MVP) achievement badges to their users. Each week and for each project known to the site, the most active committer of the project earns the badge.

In addition to developer and project profiles, the site randomly displays some of the most active developers on its front page. An ordered list of the 95 most active developers acts as a simple leaderboard.

Coderwall

Coderwall was founded in 2011 by Matthew Deiters. As of March 1st 2012, more than 15,000 users had registered with the site.

Similar to Masterbranch, Coderwall analyzes the repositories of developers on social code sharing sites. It awards achievement badges to developers when certain conditions are met. For example, if a developer uses at least four different programming languages in the repositories she owns, Coderwall will award her the *Walrus* achievement badge (Fig. 5.3(a)). The *Forked* achievement is awarded if someone else forked — that is, made their own branch of — a developer's project (Fig. 5.3(b)).

(a)   (b)

Figure 5.3: *Coderwall's* Walrus *(left) and* Forked *(right) achievement badges.*

Fig. 5.4 shows a screenshot of a developer profile[17]. On top, it displays the name, current company, location, and image of the user. Below this header, there is a timeline that chronologically lists events regarding that developer: when they earned which achievement, when they gave a talk, and others.

The right side of the page displays the developer's skills. A button offers to *endorse* the developer — a low-effort mechanism that, similar to Facebook's *like*, might signal approval. Next to the button, the number of endorsements the developer has received is displayed. Finally, the profile page lists the achievements earned by the developer. During our study, Coderwall added a list of people the developer is connected with on Twitter (not pictured).

Developers registered with Coderwall may join a team, typically named after a company. For each team, the members' contributions are accumulated, resulting in an overall score for the team. This score determines the team's ranking on the Coderwall team leaderboard[18].

---

[17]Taken from `http://coderwall.com/lsinger`
[18]`http://coderwall.com/leaderboard`

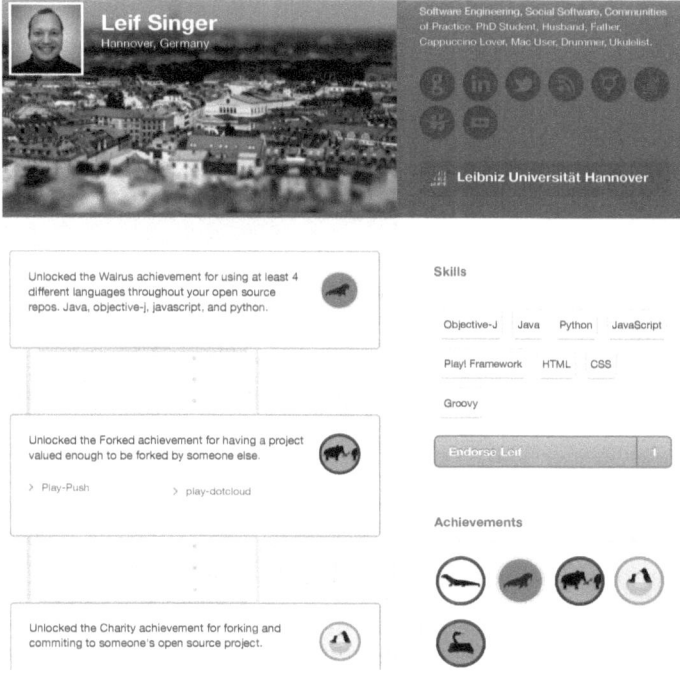

Figure 5.4: *A developer profile on Coderwall.*

5.3.2. Study Design

We use a mixed methods approach to better understand how social media, specifically tailored to software developers, can influence the developers in software engineering communities.

Research Questions

We designed a set of research questions to help us understand why software developers participate in the social programmer ecosystem, how they interact, and the impact and challenges they face.

RQ1: Why are software developers participating in the social programming ecosystem?

Software developers' public display of their development activities through social media is a relatively recent phenomenon enabled by new technology platforms. Our first research question seeks to examine the motives that software developers have for participating in this emerging ecosystem.

RQ2: How do software developers interact in the social programmer ecosystem?

Users of developer profile aggregators are constantly signaling information about themselves and their work. This information might be interpreted differently by different actors participating in the social programmer ecosystem. We are particularly interested in how software developers might be interacting with each other using profile aggregators. Research question 2 aims at examining these interactions.

RQ3: What is the impact of participating in the social programmer ecosystem?

Our third question aims to investigate the impact of participation in the ecosystem. We focus on how software developers might benefit from the environment.

RQ4: What are the risks and challenges faced by participating in the social programmer ecosystem?

Developer profiles might be interpreted differently based on differing organizational and cultural values of the participants of the social programmer ecosystem. Their interpretations may depend on community standards and conventions of practice induced by these standards [19]. Since such differences may give rise to communication problems, we investigate risks and challenges for those people using and participating in the ecosystem.

Procedures

To our knowledge, our study is the first to examine developer profile aggregators and their role in the social programmer ecosystem. As such, it is of an exploratory nature and is concerned with questions of *why* and *how*. This calls for qualitative methods, which we describe in this section.

In our study, we distributed questionnaires to Masterbranch and Coderwall users and then conducted interviews with some of them.

Questionnaires

Our instrument consisted of two web-based questionnaires: one was tailored for Masterbranch users and the other for Coderwall users. The questionnaires were equal in content and order of items, except for the terminology referencing particular features of each site. We pre-tested the questionnaire by distributing it to 10 Coderwall users, of which 5 were sampled at random and 5 were taken from the site's front page. We received responses from

3 users, and 2 of those gave feedback on the survey. After minor changes in both questionnaires (wording; additional "I don't know" options), we distributed our survey to a larger sample.

We used several forms of distribution. First, the questionnaires were advertised on Twitter by some of the authors. The operators of Masterbranch and Coderwall supported us by retweeting our invitations. Masterbranch published a blog post, inviting their users to take part in the survey. In this phase, we gathered 28 responses from Codewall users and 9 responses from Masterbranch users. To increase the number of responses, we collected the profile pages and email addresses of 315 random Coderwall members (Masterbranch does not provide random access to member profiles). We then emailed those users, inviting them to take our questionnaire. This resulted in another 46 responses.

Each form of distribution contained a URL linking to the respective questionnaire[19]. Both questionnaires were made available online using Google Forms from February 29th to April 19th 2012. Apart from an introductory cover letter, the main content sections were:

Demographics: we asked for information such as age, gender and country. We also measured respondents' professional experience in years and their current employment status, which included their primary responsibility at an organization (if employed), the organization's size and its age.

Site membership: we inquired when the respondent signed up for a profile on the respective site and asked why they did so.

Site features: for each of the features of Coderwall and Masterbranch described earlier, we asked how important they are to the respondent (on a Likert scale). We also asked some specific questions for each feature. For example, we asked respondents whether they care if people look at their profiles and what kind of profiles they are most interested in. We also asked whether they are applying explicit strategies for earning badges such as achievements on Coderwall, or the MVP on Masterbranch. Finally, we inquired about eventual strategies they might be using for earning achievements.

Responders were also asked to optionally submit their email addresses if they agreed to be contacted for an interview with our research team. In total, we received 35 responses with email addresses included, 31 of which came from Coderwall users.

---

[19]Masterbranch: `http://bitly.com/yMo22Q`; Coderwall: `http://bitly.com/zqrCo9`

Interviews

To scrutinize the answers from the survey, we invited all of the 35 survey participants who had volunteered to do interviews via email. Of these 35, 14 software developers enrolled, 2 of them from the Masterbranch survey.

We then conducted semi-structured interviews with software developers. We first asked developers about their current job situation — for example, what kind of company they work for or what the team structure is. We then used their answers from the questionnaire as a starting point for deeper inquiry, asking for the reasons and motivations for their behaviors.

Interviews were conducted mostly via Skype and were recorded; for 2 of them we used a text chat.

Participants

Overall, we received 83 responses to our questionnaires, 74 of which came from Coderwall users. 68 of the respondents were software engineers (82%), 14 were team leaders and 1 was a non-technical co-founder of a software company. We interviewed 14 software developers, among them one contractor. Table 5.2 summarizes our interview participants and lists the identifiers we assigned to them.

D1, D3-D5, D7, D8, D10-D13	employed in a software company
D6, D9, D14	consultant or contractor
D2	unemployed

Table 5.2.: *Summary of interview participants.*

Our interviewees had diverse backgrounds. To illustrate this, Table 5.3 provides a short introduction for some of the participants.

Data Analysis

We used an approach based on grounded theory for data analysis [30]. Questionnaire data was split into two data sets and two of the authors open coded each set independently. Two authors then cooperatively engaged in axial coding our preliminary set of codes and, as a result, 15 categories emerged. We used those categories to code interview data. Then, we transcribed excerpts from the interviews that were related to our research

Code	Background
D1	Developer at a Web development shop in Norway, mostly Ruby development.
D3	Developer working in an image recognition company from Spain.
D6	Developer and team coordinator in a Linux security and deployment company in the USA.
D10	Developer and team coordinator in a large software company in the USA, managing proprietary and open source efforts.
D11	Java developer for a Polish outsourcing company.

Table 5.3.: *Backgrounds of select interview participants.*

questions. The next phase comprised of selective coding over all extracted quotes (from questionnaire responses and interview transcriptions). During this process, we iterated on our previous code system and identified both the core categories and relationships that would help us answer our research questions[20].

5.3.3. Findings

This section reports the findings from the surveys and the interviews with developers. For brevity, we provide quotes only for some of the findings. The source of each quote is noted in square brackets — *[Dx]* referring to an interview with a developer; *[SMx]* and *[SCx]* to survey answers for Masterbranch and Coderwall, respectively.

RQ1: Reasons for Participation

To answer research question 1, we investigated *why* developers participate in the social programmer ecosystem.

Many software developers told us that they are ***curious about technology, passionate to learn, and always trying to improve themselves as developers***. A variation of this was given in 20 of the 83 survey answers as the reason to join one of the developer profile aggregators.

Taking part in the ecosystem allows developers to discover novelty — by joining a developer profile aggregator, publishing code on GitHub, or interacting with others on Twitter. Seeing others do interesting new things with technology ***inspires*** them. A special case are ***high-profile develop-***

---

[20]The coding system from the later phase can be found in appendix B

ers that are vocal about their technological discoveries, respected in the community, and followed by many.

"On Twitter, I follow a few prominent software developers. For example, Kelly Sommers[21] from Canada, she's constantly trying new things. I don't think she ever sleeps. She's a great source of inspiration." [D11]

A reason that was very commonly given for participation in the ecosystem was **enjoying the interactions** with other developers: *"this incredible group of fascinating people that get interested in all sorts of things, makes it interesting to talk with them, and work with them" [D1]*. This was mentioned in 8 of 14 developer interviews.

Interestingly, very few participants told us that they were looking for **competition** with regard to the number of projects, followers, or badges one has on the different social media sites. It was mentioned by 5 developers in the interviews, and only by 3 of 83 survey respondents when asked about achievements. Related to that, there was also the theme of **pride** — developers said they liked showing off their achievements and comparing themselves with others. Some specifically mentioned that they were proud of being part of a great team.

The most important reason for enjoying the community was **recognition** of others. In the survey, 19 of 83 answers with regard to the *endorsement* features of the websites were about recognition or validation of one's work. Developers like getting respect from their peers — and from random people as well — for the work they are doing. *"I would like to have some recognition from the community [...] [my projects] are fun to me, but if they are only on my hard disk then nobody knows" [D3]*

Similarly, **helping others** was also very important for several developers: *"I like to be useful to others, and this is a good way to do that" [D3]* Some explicitly said that **interacting with, and helping others, motivated them** to contribute more and to become better developers.

Finally, a few participants mentioned that they were **pushed into the ecosystem by their peers** — they had been asked to join a site or a service, and to contribute code of their own. *"I started to publish because my friends told me that [a project] didn't have any [visibility]" [D3]*

A few developers mentioned that they were striving for visibility because they were **searching for work**. Taking into account all questions of the survey, 6 of 83 respondents mentioned this. These developers said that

---

[21]https://twitter.com/kellabyte

they would like to improve their chances of being recognized by recruiters. They believe that the simplifications of experience that the developer profile aggregators provide help non-technical recruiters in assessing developers: *"I love the idea of the badges, it helps communicate to non-technical people (like recruiters) what I know" [SC14]*

RQ2: Modes and Terms of Interaction

To answer research question 2, we investigated *how* developers interact in the social programmer ecosystem.

Survey Results   Table 5.4 shows the results regarding the subjective importance of different features of the developer profile aggregators. All 83 respondents were factored in. The questions provided a Likert-type scale ranging from *1 — very important* to *5 — not important at all.* An option reading *"I don't know that feature"* was also available.

	Mean	Median	Don't know
Achievements	2.5	2.0	1
Endorsements	2.8	3.0	27
Leaderboard	3.3	3.0	15
Featured Developers	3.3	3.0	37

Table 5.4.: *Importance of the features of developer profile aggregators.*

The achievements feature, possibly being the most visible, was most important, followed by the endorsement feature. Strikingly, 37 of 83 respondents did not know the "featured developers" on the front pages of the developer profile aggregators. Supported by this additional data, we will now answer research question 2.

Many developers participate in the social programmer ecosystem to connect with others — peers, interesting people, or high-profile developers. To be able to do so, they need to **assess other developers** first.

As part of this assessment, they are investigating **what others have created**. Thus, the open source projects of developers mediate relationships in the ecosystem. They allow developers to construct a "coder footprint" of one another. *"[When] I look at repos around this topic [data visualization], I may be interested in seeing the coder footprint of people that work in this* *area [...] their favorite languages, the topics they write code about, what they work on" [D6]*

Constructing such a footprint not only helps in assessing strangers on the Internet. It is also being used to **make sense of coworkers** who might be geographically dispersed. In a similar manner, developers are using **common interests** to find interesting people and connect with them. While some developers will interact with those they discover, others choose to **passively follow** the activity of developers.

Developers are aware that their peers are assessing them as well. This leads to developers wanting to manage their *"personal brands" [D9]*, that is, consciously constructing a public image of themselves. The social programmer ecosystem is one of **mutual assessment**.

Developers enjoy and desire **recognition by peers**, which was mentioned by 11 of 14 interviewed developers: *"there's the social component. So peers — developers, coders — can see that. It gives you a good feeling when others see what I've achieved" [D12]* On the other end of this interaction, developers do recognize and **acknowledge good work**: *"I knew he worked hard in that area and felt like giving him recognition" [SC58]* This finding may be related to the relative importance of the *endorsement* feature (see Table 5.4).

RQ3: The Impact of Participation

This section reports what we found with regard to research question 3, which asks about the *impact* of participation in the social programmer ecosystem.

Our interviews revealed that the **gamification** employed by features such as Coderwall's achievements is, in fact, at least somewhat effective: *"if I need to make a repository, I'll put it on Github, it'll exist forever, and I can get a badge for it. That's really awesome. [...] It pushed me in the right direction. It forced me to play the game for the right reasons." [D13]* In our interviews, 8 of 14 developers explicitly mentioned that they felt motivated by the developer profile aggregators. This may be related to the high importance given to the achievement feature in Table 5.4.

A closer look revealed that those features **lower the barriers for participation** in developer teams and communities. As a result, opportunities for participation are more visible and tangible: *"I have been trying to get into [the open source] scene for a while, when you see an achievement that* *is available for a contribution, it is the final nudge to make an actual contribution."* [D2]

Developers also reported other reasons for participation that go beyond ludic motivations and might impact their professional progress. For instance, **learning new programming languages** is a consequence of engaging in such an environment: *"I wouldn't think of starting a repository in a specific language just to earn an achievement, but it may push me towards choosing a new language to learn"* [D6]. Also, achievements are seen as a window for **exploration and experimentation**. When asked about why achievements are important, one respondent said: *"they make me want to achieve something that I didn't know about before or open me up to new ideas."* [SC38]

The impact of such features is not limited to individuals. They **motivated whole software teams to contribute more**: *"Coderwall has generally upped the game in the office amongst our engineers. It has helped to encourage all of us to publish more code online."* [SC51]

As we saw in the findings for research question 1, developers are interested in novelty. Now we find that their drive for trying new things helps them **diffuse new ideas**. *"Generally, I sign up for every online service I think I might find interesting. [...] now our entire team is on Coderwall"* [SC51]

RQ4: Risks and Challenges of Participation

Research question 4 is concerned with potential *risks and challenges* that result from participation in the social programmer ecosystem. Backing up the necessity for this inquiry, a developer also greatly involved with recruiting told us: *"It's a new space. I think there's some value to this kind of thing [Coderwall], but I'm not sure where it is yet. Because it's a new idea."* [D10]

Many of the developers we talked to were rather isolated locally, but well-connected with weak ties on a global scale. Even though these were passionate and interested persons, they were not able to gain too much from participation in mutual assessment as implemented by developer profile aggregators: *"[Importance of leaderboard] It's not very important to me now as soon as most of my colleagues are not very interested in open source"* [SC24] They simply **lack the social connectedness** that seems to help in adopting such approaches. The relative obscurity of the *leaderboard* feature that can be seen in Table 5.4 may be related to this finding.

Even though we have found strong preferences for passionate novelty seeking, some developers mentioned that they **struggle to keep up** with their fast-paced environment. *"The whole 'what's new today thing' is exhausting"* [D1]

Because developer profile aggregators, social code sharing sites, and social media in general are very public by their nature, the actual audience of content cannot be determined beforehand. We found two conflicting views regarding this issue.

Several developers are aware that **public signals should not receive too much weight** — they mentioned that the reasons for the existence or absence of such signals can be very different from what people might assume. As a developer involved with recruiting told us, *"The GitHub repository doesn't show everything though. I wouldn't discard someone with an emptyish GitHub repo. Might just show that most of his/her projects were closed-source. That's why nothing can replace a few emails."* [D4]

5.3.4. Discussion

In this section, we discuss some of the most important themes that emerged from our study and their potential impact on software engineering practice.

Mutual Assessment

The core category that we found in our study was that of *mutual assessment*: developers continually used social media to assess each other. For this, the high degree of social transparency [171] in the social programmer ecosystem provides novel reputation signals, and known signals that are being used in novel ways. The aggregation performed by sites such as Masterbranch and Coderwall helps in quantifying the activities of the programmers in the ecosystem, and it also enables the creation of symbols for certain kinds of participation in the ecosystem.

For the developers we studied, everything revolves around their passion for technology and learning, as well as being connected to other passionate developers. Thus, they assess each other in terms of the technologies they use and the problems they solve, using each others' *coder footprint* (see below) with the goal of finding new stimuli and collaborators.

Developers use the signals in the ecosystem to assess companies as well: *"I want to gauge the quality of developers in a certain organization, so I can determine if I'm a good fit for a position there."* The presence of a company's developers in the social programmer ecosystem is an indication of that company's philosophy with regard to using the latest technology and participating in open source.

We suspect that this mutual assessment in the social programmer ecosystem may be supporting the dissemination and adoption of technology and software development practices. According to Rogers' *innovation-decision process* [149], to adopt an innovation, individuals first need to gain knowledge of it. The second step of that process is *persuasion*, the formation of a favorable or unfavorable attitude towards the innovation. Both processes are heavily influenced by opinion leadership. As we saw in our research, the social programmer ecosystem supports the formation of such authorities — e.g. through several reputation-relevant signals — and provides different communication channels through which to diffuse information about innovations. The mutual assessment may help creating, judging, and finding opinion leaders.

Related to this, Murphy-Hill and Murphy [124] show that developers learn about new technology from chance encounters with peers. Draxler and Stevens [52] studied how Eclipse users appropriate plug-ins, distinguishing between need-driven and opportunity-driven appropriation. We see equivalents to these modes in discovery processes in social media — need-driven and opportunity-driven discovery. Nardi [126] found similar processes when studying Communities of Practice [103] of spreadsheet users. Individuals who were known for their expertise — coined *gardeners* or *tinkerers* — were approached by less proficient users about problem solutions and innovations. In our study, we saw hints that the high degree of social transparency in the social programmer ecosystem may support both serendipitous discoveries and targeted searches for solutions — however, without the requirement for physical proximity. Stack Overflow with its Q&A format seems to produce very need-driven content. On Twitter, both forms are supported: members passively follow trustable sources for opportunity-driven discovery and actively interact with others for need-driven discovery. Sites like Masterbranch and Coderwall support almost no direct interaction between users, concentrating on creating opportunities for serendipitous discoveries.

Passion

The core aim of mutual assessment, we found, was identifying *passion* in others. This passion appears to be the main motivation for programmers to participate in the ecosystem. The participants in our surveys and interviews love programming and creating things. The applications used in the social programmer ecosystem and their features make it easy for them to find interesting potential collaborators as well as interesting new technologies to learn. In that sense, the signals of the ecosystem are a mechanism to reduce uncertainty about technologies as well as other actors.

Developer profile aggregators are a vehicle for programmers to showcase themselves and their achievements. The focus is not on job hunting, but rather on having fun, building something cool, and generally *"being awesome"* — as one of our survey respondents put it. Developers use profile aggregators to show their peers and potential collaborators how passionate they are and that they love what they do, connecting them with each other.

As reported by Vallerand et al. [183], passion and performance are deeply connected. Therefore it makes sense for developers in the social programmer ecosystem to be looking for passionate individuals: these are more likely to perform better as colleagues in companies or as collaborators in open source projects. Specifically for the latter, Wu et al. [195] found that high motivation — for which passion may be a sign — may influence future engagement in open source software projects, helping others in deciding which potential employees or collaborators might be most valuable to invest in.

Coder Footprint

In several interviews with developers, the interviewees struggled to say exactly what they were looking for in other developers. Some wished to *"get a better picture"*, others wanted to *"get a feel"* for what kind of developer the other person was. They all agreed, however, that multiple factors are important: the developer's technical niche and its popularity in the community; their diversity; their passion for technology; their standing in the community. Quoting one of our interviewees, we call this their *coder footprint*. While sites such as GitHub are also suitable, developer profile aggregators in particular provide a condensed representation of the coder footprint that can be grasped quickly.

Grasping the coder footprint seems to be the primary function of the profile aggregators. Developers claimed to be trying to get a feel for what other developers were about.

The coder footprint serves an important purpose in the social programmer ecosystem. Developers are driven by a passion for new technologies, new ideas, and learning. The coder footprint allows them to navigate a vast social space much more easily, supporting them in their search for novelty and social connectedness. While sites are still experimenting on how to get the coder footprint right, and several interviewees voiced criticism and concerns regarding the validity of the signals found on developer profile aggregators, the current iteration is an already useful glimpse at what future developers might be using to assess and explore each other.

As argued by Funder [67], any accuracy when judging the personalities of others *"stems from the relevance, availability, detection, and utilization of behavioral cues."* The social transparency [171] found on sites and services of the social programmer ecosystem provides for many such cues. For example, an interviewee also involved with recruiting explicitly mentioned that he watches how potential hires behave on public mailing lists and in issue discussions on GitHub — an application of *interaction transparency* for assessment. The coder footprint as a simplification of such behavior seems to be a useful construct helping with the aforementioned mutual assessment.

Diversity

Developers were regarded as *diverse* when they were perceived as interested in multiple technologies, ideally with different characteristics. Especially very current technologies — such as Clojure or NodeJS — and those requiring different modes of thinking — e.g. object-oriented vs. functional programming languages — were used as signals for diversity. Developers tried to become more diverse as part of their personal improvement efforts and also looked for it in other developers.

We believe this might be an indicator for a cultural change in software development. Proficiency in a certain niche is no longer enough, as developers are expected to be able to easily adapt to a changing technology landscape. Developers expect it from others as potential collaborators or sources of interesting information, and also from themselves.

Several parties might be interested in leveraging this insight. Developers that are aware of it might take it as a motivation to become more diverse themselves. Others might try exploiting the potential for manipulation, for example by creating many repositories containing trivial projects in several programming languages. Developer training — for example at universities — is already somewhat diverse in that it mostly teaches concepts instead of concrete programming languages. However, these are often restricted to only one or two programming paradigms, such as object-oriented programming. Taking a cue from software development practitioners, universities might want to support their students in attaining a higher level of diversity.

While most participants of our study used diversity in programming languages as a signal for actual diversity and adaptability, there might be other, more appropriate measures for this character trait. A few interviewees stressed the importance of public communication, for example on Twitter, to help in assessing this. Therefore, tag clouds and badges of programming languages might just be a first iteration of a more important idea — simplifying the assessment of diversity in developers.

As Ye and Kishida report [196], learning is an important motivation of open source developers. Diversity as a signal for being able to learn different concepts seems like a good way to gauge the motivation of a developer. Therefore, similar to passion, diversity may be an appropriate surrogate for assessing others' motivations. Again, social transparency in the social programmer ecosystem makes suitable signals publicly available.

Impact

Our findings indicate the presence of novel dynamics between developers in the social programmer ecosystem, enabled by an unprecedented social transparency in the software engineering domain. These dynamics may have multiple positive as well as negative impacts.

The software developers we talked to viewed participation in social media and mutual developer assessment in a largely positive light. For them, it presents opportunities to learn about new technologies and to connect with other like-minded people who they might not be able to find locally in their own organizations. Several developers also spoke of how participating in the social programmer ecosystem and knowing that other developers were following their activities propelled them to contribute more or better quality code, and to improve themselves as developers. This effect has been shown for GitHub by Dabbish et al. [38].

This study explores how a group of early adopter software developers are interacting with new social media platforms. As such, the question arises as to whether and how these trends extrapolate to the rest of the software development community. Software developers outside the early adopters group may find many of the same benefits in using social media as part of their development activities. However, motivations for participation by this group may well differ from those of the early adopters.

There is also the issue of developers feeling compelled to participate in the ecosystem to keep up with expectations of the wider software development community. Many developers are not able to participate freely in social media due to their employment circumstances; others may be dissuaded by the potential for public criticism of their work. A future developer landscape that expects a public portfolio of work available for contribution or participation in the community could have the unintended consequence of isolating these developers from the community rather than connecting them to it.

5.3.5. Limitations

We used a Grounded Theory approach, which involved conducting surveys and semi-structured interviews, and coding of the results from these. These methods do not allow us to infer statistical significance of our findings. However, these methods are well-suited for exploration and discovery and can suggest how and why developers participate in the social programmer ecosystem. As this is the first study on the role of developer profile aggregators, we consider these methods and their focus on exploration to be suitable for our purposes.

The responses to our questionnaires and interviews came exclusively from members of the Coderwall and Masterbranch sites, as these were the most visible when we started our research. Participants in both the questionnaires and the interviews were self-selected by volunteering for them. Therefore, the responses are naturally biased. We found that many developers exhibited traits of the *innovators* adopter category as defined by Rogers [149]: with only few local ties, they were connected globally with many weak ties and used those to bring new ideas and technologies into their own local societies — Rogers calls them *venturesome*. This character trait may have helped with the relatively good response rates for the questionnaires and interviews (e.g., 35 of 83 total respondents offered to do an interview, of which 14 were realized). Even before sending out personal invitations to members of Coderwall, most responses came from members of Coderwall instead of Masterbranch. That might be explained by the relatively high media exposure the site had recently[22].

Another limitation of this study lies in the relatively low number of interviews conducted. However, we were able to increase the credibility and validity of our findings by triangulating data from interviews and survey responses. Also, the interviewees had a wide range of different backgrounds, allowing us to consider many different perspectives in this work.

The current users of developer profile aggregators are *innovators* and *early adopters*, and thus are not representative of the entire software developer population. However, they allow us to gain early insights into the role of profile aggregators in the ecosystem of social programmers, and to shed light on the potential impact of these sites on software developers.

Coderwall and Masterbranch are among the first sites to aggregate developer data across various social media developer services. As more individuals start using these sites and other services emerge, additional studies should be conducted to gain further insights into the complex ecosystem of social programmers.

5.3.6. Conclusions

We discussed a group of software developers that are using new social media tools to communicate and share their development activity with fellow developers. These developers, their motivations, and the technology infrastructure they use combine to produce an ecosystem where open collaboration and public sharing of who you are and what you do is ingrained.

Our findings indicate that the developers we surveyed are motivated by a strong passion for discovery and learning about new software development technologies. To satisfy this need, they explore the technology landscape through the prism of other like-minded developers' activities and coder footprints. They are aware of other developers and actively assess and are assessed by them. This process is facilitated and encouraged by the underlying technology infrastructure of the social programmer ecosystem, which places its emphasis not on software projects, but rather on software developers and their activities across multiple projects and communities.

Across the different social media sites we encountered in our study, we found several mechanisms that could be appropriated to support the adoption of software engineering practices. Developers enjoy the playful nature

---

[22]http://techcrunch.com/2012/02/27/coderwall-hacker-reputation-system/

of this ecosystem. They use Twitter to follow opinion leaders and to connect with one another. Their peers and social media mechanisms such as achievement badges can motivate them to try out new technologies and practices.

5.4. Summary

This chapter first showed that the adoption of software engineering practices can be problematic. Even though processes and tools are in place that aim at improving adoption, individual developers sometimes still do not comply even with mandated practices. Because of the positive effects software engineering practices can have, this is undesirable for organizations involved with software development.

The chapter then reported on two studies on the use of social media in software development: first concentrating on the adoption of testing practices on the social coding site GitHub, providing insights into adoption problems regarding testing practices and into strategies that can alleviate these problems. Secondly, this chapter investigated developer profile aggregators and how developers use them and other social media tools to assess each other. Both studies indicate that social media and insights from human-computer interaction could be used to address problems of practice adoption.

For example, in the study of developer profile aggregators, we found that virtual badges can push software developers to try out new technologies. The study on testing practices in GitHub found that providing easy access to test code helps in communicating testing as a social norm, persuading others to imitate this behavior. The next chapter introduces a process to systematically use such effects to improve the adoption of software engineering practices by developers in an organization.

6. Supporting Practice Adoption in Software Engineering

As shown in the previous chapter, the adoption of software engineering practices is a problem. Yet, some approaches exist that improve the adoption of practices — even if this simply means pushing a developer to try a practice for the first time.

However, these approaches do not seem to be guided by a systematic approach, and are not easily reproducible by others. GitHub, Masterbranch, and Coderwall for example are private enterprises. It is therefore not clear whether they have applied any systematic method for building their systems in a way that emphasizes features that can have a positive effect on practice adoption. Even if they have: their approach is not public. Therefore, such a systematic approach that shows how to use these effects for improving the adoption of software engineering practices is missing.

After first defining several relevant terms, this chapter introduces a process that explains how *change agents* in organizations can systematically design treatments for persuasive interventions that improve the adoption of a practice by their developers. To avoid lengthy repetitions and ambiguities, the process is called the *Practice Adoption Improvement Process* and is abbreviated as *PAIP*. To apply this process, the change agent will need a set of *adoption patterns* for designing the aforementioned treatments — these are provided by chapter 7. Chapter 8 evaluates a preliminary version of the process and the accompanying patterns.

6.1. Definitions

This thesis provides a process that enables an organization to improve the adoption of software engineering practices by the organization's software developers. In the process, a change agent chooses adoption patterns that support the change agent's adoption goal by mitigating the organization's adoption problem in a persuasive manner. Based on these patterns, the change agent designs a treatment and deploys it in the organization as a persuasive intervention.

To clarify the meaning of the preceding paragraph, this section introduces some relevant terms. They also support the explanation of the process in the succeeding section. Some terms may have different meanings outside of this thesis.

Definition 9: Organization.

An organization is a social entity that has a collective goal. Reaching that goal involves writing software, and some or all members of the organization are software developers. Optionally, each member of the organization is part of one or more groups inside the organization. Such groups can imply a hierarchical order.

In accordance with definition 9, an organization can e.g. be a company with a software development department, a loosely assembled team, or an open source project. All of these provide a valid context for the application of this thesis' results.

Definition 10: Software Engineering Practice.

A software engineering practice is a set of systematic activities that are expected to have an influence on non-functional properties of the software produced by developers applying the practice or on the process of developing the software.

An example for a software engineering practice as defined in definition 10 is test-driven development (TDD). It has been shown to lower the defect rate of software products in several cases [125]. Other examples are the use of a version control system, different systems that prescribe *how* to commit to version control[1], or documentation that might be required for compliance with policies of partners or government institutions, improving a software products marketability or enabling it in the first place. Section 5.1.1 provides additional examples for valuable software engineering practices.

---

[1]See, e.g., a blog post advertising committing *frequently*: `http://ducquoc.wordpress.com/2011/06/09/svn-best-practices/`

PAIP is performed by a role called the *change agent*. Adapted from Rogers' [149] definition, this thesis defines the change agent as follows.

Definition 11: Change Agent.

A change agent *is a member of an organization who influences the organization's developers' innovation-decisions in a direction deemed desirable by the organization. The change agent seeks to improve the adoption of practices.*

(cf. Rogers [149])

The change agent strives to solve the organization's *adoption problems*. In a software development company, the change agent role might e.g. be occupied by a development process manager or a person responsible for development process governance. Within the scope of this thesis, a change agent's goals are always related to *improving* the adoption of software engineering practices.

Definition 12: Adoption Problem.

An adoption problem *is a situation in which the desired and the actual adoption of a software engineering practice in an organization differ. The organization acknowledges that a reduction of the difference is desired and supports efforts aimed at reducing the difference.*

Within the scope of this thesis, an organization is assumed to support the change agent's goals. An example for an adoption problem can be found in chapter 8: in a student project, developers tended not to commit frequently enough and often did not enter any commit messages, making it harder to understand a project's development history later.

To attempt to solve adoption problems, the change agent uses PAIP and, in one of the process' steps, chooses a set of *adoption patterns* to apply.

Definition 13: Adoption Pattern.

An adoption pattern *documents the abstract core of a known solution to a recurring adoption problem. Instantiations of an adoption pattern are tailored to a specific problem they are supposed to solve, so that two instantiations will usually differ.* *(cf. Alexander [4])*

This definition is based on Alexander's design patterns from architecture [4], which were later popularized in software development by Gamma et al. [69]. Using PAIP and a set of adoption patterns, the change agent will try to reach an *adoption goal*.

Definition 14: Adoption Goal.

An adoption goal *is a change in the adoption of a software engineering practice desired by the organization. The organization has assigned competence to the change agent to act upon the adoption goal.*

Regarding the aforementioned adoption problem documented in chapter 8, adoption goals were to increase the commit frequency of developers and to increase the length of commit messages.

As part of PAIP, the change agent uses the adoption patterns to design a *treatment*:

Definition 15: Treatment.

A treatment *is software that was designed or commissioned by a change agent, deliberately instantiates adoption patterns, and is aimed at reaching an adoption goal.*

Deploying one or more treatments in an organization is a *persuasive intervention*:

Definition 16: Persuasive Intervention.

A persuasive intervention *is the deployment of one or more treatments by — or commissioned by — a change agent, aimed at reaching an adoption goal in a non-coercive attempt to change attitudes and / or behaviors.*

Synonyms: intervention; PAIP intervention.

(cf. Fogg et al. [62])

PAIP focuses on persuasive interventions as an alternative to mandating behavior, as the latter is not always followed [146]. Persuasion also has other advantages: in line with Self-determination Theory, perceived autonomy has been shown to improve the well-being of employees, in turn improving their creativity and productivity [6].

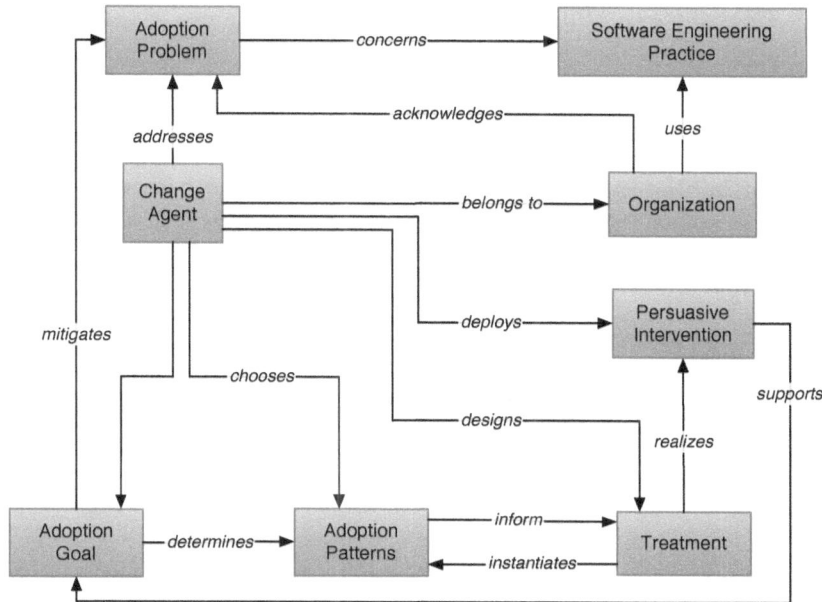

Figure 6.1: *The defined terms and their relationships.*

Fig. 6.1 provides an overview of the basic terms defined in this section. Based on these, the following section defines the actual process.

6.2. PAIP: The Practice Adoption Improvement Process

This section introduces PAIP, the Practice Adoption Improvement Process. PAIP consists of six steps that the change agent executes in an iterative cycle. The process allows her to systematically create and improve persuasive interventions that are aimed at improving the adoption of software engineering methods in an organization.

PAIP is inspired by the Quality Improvement Paradigm by Basili et al. (cf. Basili et al.'s Experience Factory [11]) and Deming's [47] Plan-Do-Check-Act (PDCA) cycle. It is a continuous process that aims at lowering the discrepancy between the current situation and the adoption goal with each iteration. While PAIP can be used on its own, organizations with other software process improvement (SPI) initiatives in place could integrate PAIP into their existing efforts.

First, I provide an overview of PAIP's six steps:

1. ***Characterize Context:*** In this first step, the change agent determines the current context in which PAIP is to be applied. This entails the practice for which adoption should be improved as well as its properties, and the characteristics of the developer population.

2. ***Define Adoption Goal & Metrics:*** Using established paradigms such as the Goal/Question/Metric method (GQM) [185], the change agent defines the adoption goal that the intervention should be optimized for. PAIP constrains the goal to a specific set of classes (see below) to enable a mapping to concrete adoption patterns. To measure success in step 6, the change agent defines metrics. These can also be incorporated into the treatment design, as several patterns need metrics to provide different kinds of feedback to developers.

3. ***Choose Adoption Patterns:*** In the previous two steps, the change agent has collected the information necessary to choose the adoption patterns that are appropriate for her context and adoption goal.

4. ***Design Treatment:*** Using the adoption patterns chosen in the previous step, the change agent can now design one or more software applications that implement the patterns. Each adoption pattern lists implementation examples that the change agent can use to base her treatment on.

5. ***Deploy Intervention:*** Once the treatments have been created, the change agent deploys them as a persuasive intervention in the organization.

6. ***Analyze Results:*** When the intervention is deployed, its effects can be measured using the metrics defined in step 2. By comparing these measurements with a baseline measurement, the intervention's success is assessed. This step provides data to guide the next iteration of the process.

Fig. 6.2 provides an overview of the process. The following sections discuss these steps in detail.

Step 1: Characterize Context

At the beginning of the process, the change agent knows about an adoption problem related to a software engineering practice. She has already ensured

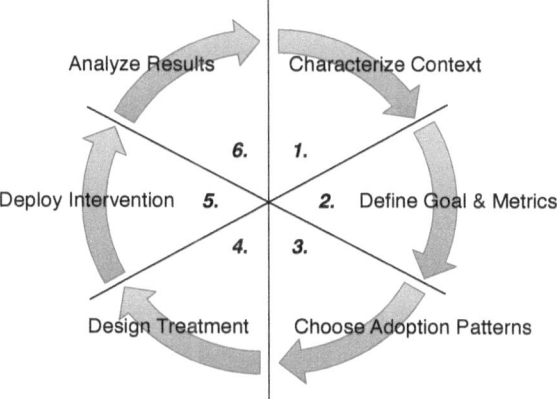

Figure 6.2: *An overview of the Practice Adoption Improvement Process.*

that the problem really is related to adoption issues and is not caused by other reasons, such as missing resources or management buy-in.

The change agent then determines key characteristics of the software engineering practice for which adoption is to be improved and the developer population of the organization.

The Software Engineering Practice

In the context of PAIP, a software engineering practice is characterized by the tasks it entails. The majority of a practice's tasks are either *creative* or *routine*. If no clear majority can be determined, the conservative default should be to assume *creative* tasks.

This is a very simplistic model, but it supports choosing suitable adoption patterns in step 3 of PAIP. Some of the patterns use extrinsic motivators — as such, they are only appropriate for pushing developers to try something new, or for improving engagement with *routine* tasks. For creative tasks, individuals often also have intrinsic motivators — however, adding extrinsic motivators to such tasks can diminish existing intrinsic motivation (cf. chapter 3).

Determining whether a practice's tasks are creative or routine can only be an approximation, as the "truth" will likely vary between individuals applying the practice. However, as a rule of thumb, routine tasks tend to be simpler and more repetitive. This level of accuracy has so far been sufficient for using PAIP (cf. chapter 8).

The Developer Population

For the developer population of the organization, PAIP uses a similarly simple model: either some developers are already applying the practice to a desirable degree or not. Again, this information is needed when choosing adoption patterns in step 3. Some adoption patterns use existing adopters as role models that other developers can learn from. Therefore, this characteristic determines which adoption patterns might not be applicable.

Step 2: Define Adoption Goal & Metrics

The change agent has now determined the context in which PAIP is applied. The second step is concerned with the goal of the intervention. The change agent needs to answer the following questions with regard to the goal:

- What is the adoption goal?

- Which adoption goal class does the adoption goal belong to?

- Which metrics are appropriate for measuring effectiveness?

- When will effectiveness be measured?

The following sections discuss these questions in detail.

Defining the Adoption Goal

Using established paradigms such as the Goal/Question/Metric method (GQM) [185], the change agent defines the adoption goal that the intervention should be optimized for.

It has been beneficial to choose goals that are not too far from the current adoption levels of the developer populations (cf. chapter 8). Reaching the adoption goal should be a moderate step towards better adoption. Further improvements can still be gained in future iterations of PAIP. This is also in line with insights documented by Rogers [149]: reaching moderate adoption goals first can support reaching larger adoption goals later, as adoption is always also determined by the compatibility of an innovation with an individual's current practices and values. Such small steps are less demanding on potential adopters, as adoption requires only smaller changes in behavior.

A strategy that can be combined with this approach is mentioned by Gilbert [72] and was also successfully applied in the quasi-experiment documented in chapter 8: when striving to improve the competence of an organization's members, the highest gains can be achieved by targeting the worst performers. The adoption goal thus should first target those developers not using the practice at all or those using it incorrectly. Again, later iterations of PAIP can build on such improvements to introduce more advanced adoption goals.

Adoption Goal Classes

PAIP constrains the goal to one of two possible adoption goal classes (cf. definition 17).

Definition 17: Adoption Goal Class.

An adoption goal's adoption goal class determines which adoption patterns are suitable to reach the adoption goal. It can either one or both of the following.

- **Start Adopting a New Practice:** *Developers are not experienced with the tasks that are needed to apply this practice and should start applying it.*

- **Improve Adoption of a Known Practice:** *Developers have already started using the practice, but the change agent wants to improve how intensively they apply it. This entails increasing quality, frequency, duration, or volume.*

This simple model for categorizing the adoption goal enables a mapping to adoption patterns in step 3 of PAIP.

To determine how diffused the practice already is, the change agent must take a baseline measurement. Obtaining this and further measurements are discussed next.

The Appropriateness of Metrics

To determine the degree of success for an intervention and for planning consecutive PAIP iterations, the change agent derives metrics that measure adoption — that is, the degree of practice conformance as implemented by the developers. Again, existing methods such as GQM [185] should be used.

These metrics can also be incorporated into the treatment design, as several adoption patterns need metrics to provide different kinds of feedback to developers. In order to provide realtime feedback to developers, measurements should be automated.

When using metrics for monitoring and managing software development processes, a change agent can make several mistakes. Bouwers et al. [18] provide an overview of typical problems, such as *"Metric in a bubble"* or *"Treating the metric"*.

While such warnings apply, PAIP is especially concerned with the human side of metrics — the effects metrics can have on developers. Several adoption patterns use metrics to provide feedback, as a reward, or as a symbol for reputation or proficiency (cf. e.g. the *Leaderboard* or *Progress Feedback* patterns). The change agent needs to especially consider the following three issues in this context.

- *Meaning:* metrics, when used as feedback or for rewards, are more effective when they are perceived as meaningful by individuals [99].

- *Manipulation:* whenever a metric is used for rewards or to rank individuals against each other, they may attempt to manipulate its calculation. Campbell [24] enumerates several examples for this from public policy setting.

- *Playfulness:* when a metric can have concrete, material effects, the probability for it to become corrupted increases [24] — e.g. when it is used to determine salaries or promotions. Therefore, metrics in PAIP should be playful and have no real-world impacts (cf. also chapter 3 on the effect of evaluations).

Some of the adoption patterns in chapter 7 require a meaningful metric to be available. Therefore, the change agent needs to know beforehand whether the chosen metric is perceived as meaningful. While there is no formula for determining meaning, a transparent calculation of the metric and whether it reflects actual accomplishments are good indicators for estimating this. For validation, the change agent should communicate with the developer population.

For example, in the quasi-experiment documented in chapter 8, my colleagues and I used a very simple, meaningless metric to rank developers against each other: the number of commits to version control. In interviews we conducted after the project, participants told us that they perceived the metric as arbitrary and useless [164]. Some participants also remarked that this metric was prone to manipulation — however, no developer actually attempted this.

Therefore, in another iteration of the project, we would have chosen a metric that would be more meaningful. From our experience, communicating with the developer population about the chosen metrics can be a useful tool to determine whether a metric is perceived as meaningful — some students proposed test coverage, for example. Finally, the *Review* and *Meta-Review* patterns can be used to conduct potentially more meaningful measurements (cf. chapter 7).

Planning Measurement

Before deploying the persuasive intervention, the change agent uses the metrics gathered so far to make a baseline measurement of the current state of adoption. This enables her to later assess whether the intervention was successful and, in turn, which next steps would be appropriate in future iterations of PAIP. Ideally, the baseline measurement consists of multiple measurements, entailing the whole period for which future measurements are planned. Depending on the organization's process, milestones, sprints, iterations, or whole projects can be appropriate periods for taking measurements.

Depending on the organization's resources and the metrics' complexity, automatic measurement can enable realtime measurements. Generally, gathering more data is better. However, change agents should refrain from making judgements based on the data from only a short period. For all interventions, novelty can be a facilitating factor. Therefore, to obtain reliable measurements, some time should be allowed to pass. Interviewing developers from time to time may help to determine whether novelty is still affecting the intervention.

Step 3: Choose Adoption Patterns

In the previous steps, the change agent has collected the following information:

1. Is the adoption goal to *start* or to *improve* adoption for a practice?

2. Does the practice emphasize *creative* or *routine* tasks?

3. Are there *existing adopters* available that could serve as role models?

4. Is a *meaningful metric* available?

This information can be used to choose appropriate adoption patterns from Table 7.1 in chapter 7. Adoption patterns are grouped by the stages of the innovation-decision process they support. The change agent should aim at choosing a pattern from each of the stages, so developers in all stages can be supported. Fig. 6.3 illustrates how each pattern category supports a specific stage or problem in the innovation-decision process.

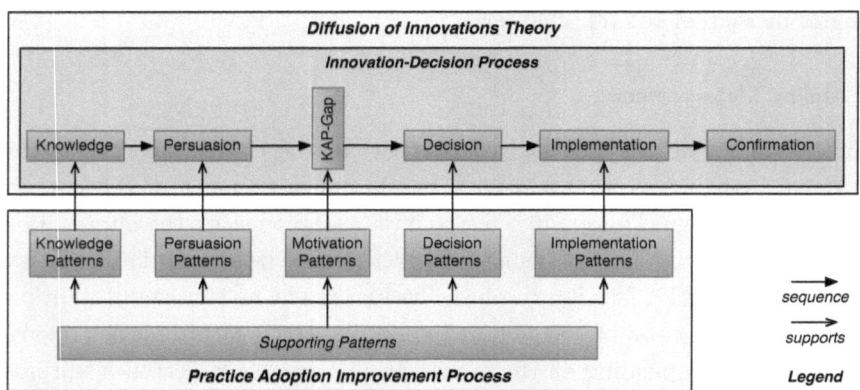

Figure 6.3: *The adoption pattern categories and their relationships to Diffusion of Innovations theory.*

However, the succeeding section will show that small, focused, and integrated treatments are preferable to larger ones. The change agent should therefore rather choose fewer adoption patterns than would be applicable.

Step 4: Design Treatment

Based on the adoption patterns the change agent has chosen in the previous process step, she can now design one or more treatments that will comprise the persuasive intervention. Each pattern contains an *Examples* section — this can be used to guide the concrete implementations of the adoption patterns.

PAIP recommends designing small, focused treatments and integrating them with existing practices and tools. Developers should be able to connect with each other in small-world networks so network effects have the most impact. The following sections discuss these issues in more detail.

Focused Treatments

As a platform for the exploration of effects in social network sites, Peters [138] and Singer [163] created *Hallway*, an extensible social network site. A single installation of Hallway can serve multiple client organizations, providing tailored social media features for each, and making many different data sources available for integration.

For example, members might be able to connect with each other only mutually, or follow others one-sidedly. For one client, members would be able to *repost* others' content; for another one there would only be the option to *like* someone else's content. Users can integrate version control repositories, bug trackers, and RSS feeds to generate posts in a user's activity stream.

Through an exploratory evaluation of *Hallway* in a student project, we learned that such large and capable interventions are very hard to keep effective. Users would be confused and overwhelmed by the available options. Only very few actually discovered which data sources they could integrate. The versatility of Hallway seemed to be hindering its adoption.

When creating *Teamfeed* — the intervention documented in chapter 8 — we took the opposite approach. Teamfeed is a simple website with only a single view: the feed of one's team members' commits to version control, along with a high-score list[2]. Users did not have to integrate their repositories themselves, or even register for the site. This approach of low barriers led to a satisfactory adoption of the intervention itself, resulting in an improvement of the software engineering practice targeted by the intervetion (cf. chapter 8). The power of lowering barriers was also confirmed in the study Pham et al. [140] conducted on GitHub (cf. chapter 5).

Another advantage of focused treatments lies in their development. Smaller treatments should take less time to develop and to improve, supporting the iterative nature of PAIP.

Therefore, PAIP recommends that the change agent focuses a treatment on a single aspect and removes as many barriers to adoption as possible.

---

[2]also called *leaderboard*

Process & Tool Integration

According to Favre et al. [59], to ensure adoption of tools by software engineers — such as our PAIP interventions — they should be integrated into existing tools and practices. For software developers, the authors specifically mention the Web, email, and integrated development environments (IDEs). PAIP therefore recommends creating treatments as integrations into existing web applications (such as bug trackers) or as self-contained web applications.

We applied the latter approach successfully in the quasi-experiment documented in chapter 8. Others have integrated social features into IDEs (e.g. Guzzi and Begel [81]) — however, depending on the organization, the required development effort might be higher and portability might be lower for IDE integration. Girgensohn and Lee [73] argue that web applications can be updated especially easily, enabling the change agent to respond quickly to usage patterns. The change agent will need to balance the advantages and disadvantages of these approaches individually.

Email should be used for notifications and triggers, as e.g. recommended by the *Triggers* pattern (cf. chapter 8). Girgensohn and Lee [73] also recommend using email notifications to motivate users to return to a web application.

Sellen et al. [160] provide further insights into how knowledge workers use the web, providing support for web- and email-based approaches. Further, Bertram et al. [15] show that social web applications can support communication and coordination even in co-located teams.

In the context of diffusion of innovations research, such an integrated approach increases the *compatibility* of interventions with existing tools and practices, which is positively correlated with adoption. Integration into existing tools and practices also spares developers of having to install new software, which increases the *trialability* of the intervention — a characteristic that is also positively correlated with adoption. The adoption of the intervention — a meta-adoption in the context of PAIP — is necessary for the intervention to have an effect.

Small-World Networks

Finally, the change agent should encourage and support the formation of small-world networks through the intervention. In such networks, nodes form clusters, and from each cluster, only a few nodes have connections to other clusters. Social networks — that is, human actors and the ties between them — as well as some other real-world phenomena are small-world networks.

Several adoption patterns, such as *Normative Behavior* or *Social Anchor* use social network effects. Various authors have shown that small-world networks support such effects well. For example, Centola [26] reports on an experiment that showed that small-world networks as compared with other network configurations show a higher degree of what the author calls "social contagion" — the adoption of behavior observed in one's peers.

Goel et al. [76] specifically mention adoption effects in their study of several online communities. According to the authors, adoption mostly takes place very near the source of a behavior and does not get carried very far between nodes. Sun et al. [175] present similar findings for popular posts on Facebook.

To support the formation of such networks, developers should be able to choose their connections themselves, e.g. by allowing them to "follow" each other's activity as proposed by the *Microblog* adoption pattern. Seeding and recommendation approaches to create connections between users have also been successful: for example, Kwan and Damian [97] show how email archives can be used to obtain social connections that would otherwise be hidden. Freyne et al. [65] show how recommending social connections early can increase engagement with a social network site.

Step 5: Deploy Intervention

The change agent now deploys the persuasive intervention in the organization. While this may entail technical tasks like provisioning computing resources or organizational duties such as obtaining permission from superiors, those activities are outside this thesis' scope. The change agent communicates to developers how the intervention will affect them and how it can help them improve their practice adoption.

Step 6: Analyze Results

When the intervention is deployed, the change agent measures its effects using the metrics she defined before, comparing these measurements against the baseline and the adoption goal. She uses the periods defined in step 2 to time such comparisons.

From our experience (cf. chapter 8), qualitative insights into the perceptions of an interventions can be valuable for guiding intervention improvements as well. The LID approach [156] is a very light-weight technique to conduct such investigations.

When the change agent has assessed the effects of the intervention, she can use the next PAIP iteration to either correct problems, to introduce further improvements to the adoption of the chosen software engineering practice, or focus it on another practice. As Thom et al. [178] argue, novelty effects could be used by constantly introducing change in the intervention.

6.3. Summary

This chapter presented PAIP, the Practice Adoption Improvement Process. By deriving the adoption context, an adoption goal, and accompanying metrics, the change agent is enabled to choose adoption patterns suited for the adoption problem. Using the adoption patterns, the change agent designs a treatment and deploys it as a persuasive intervention. The change agent then uses the metrics defined before to measure the effectiveness of the intervention. With this information, the change agent can then adapt the intervention to become more effective in improving the adoption of the chosen software engineering practice — starting the process anew.

However, a crucial part of the process is still missing: the adoption patterns that guide the design of the treatments. The next chapter presents them in detail.

7. A Catalog of Adoption Patterns

The previous chapter introduced a process called PAIP for improving the adoption of software engineering practices. To do so, step 3 of PAIP requires a change agent to choose *adoption patterns* (cf. definition 13) that match with the adoption problem, the adoption goal, the software engineering practice for which adoption should be improved, and the developer population. This chapter first documents the stages of the innovation-decision process supported by the available adoption patterns. It then reports on the procedure that was used to derive adoption patterns, and then documents the patterns themselves.

7.1. Introduction

The goal of applying PAIP is supporting the innovation diffusion process to facilitate the adoption of practices. It is therefore guided by the innovation-decision process for individuals. However, as mentioned in chapter 6, PAIP is concerned with adoption issues in organizations. As shown in chapter 2, in this case the innovation process for organizations is important to consider as well. It entails the following stages:

1. *Agenda-Setting:* The organization identifies and prioritizes needs and problems that could be addressed by adopting an innovation.

2. *Matching:* The problem identified in the previous stage is matched with an innovation could solve it.

3. *Redefining / Restructuring:* The organization customizes the innovation according to its own structure, culture, and needs.

4. *Clarifying:* Use of the innovation is starting to diffuse in the organization. The meaning of the innovation becomes clearer for the organization's members, and they start forming a common understanding of it.

5. *Routinizing:* The innovation loses its distinct quality; it is now part of the organization.

PAIP assumes that the software engineering practice to adopt has already been researched and decided upon by the organization. Therefore, the *clarifying* and *routinizing* stages (printed bold above) are relevant. In these stages, individual members of the organization adopt the practice. To support these stages, PAIP refers to the innovation-decision process for individuals which is again summarized below.

1. **Knowledge:** An individual becomes aware of an innovation and gains knowledge about how to apply it. Mass media and interpersonal networks serve as communication channels in this stage.

2. **Persuasion:** The individual forms an attitude towards the innovation. This is influenced by the properties of the innovation, by the opinions of peers, and several other factors.

    a) **KAP-gap:** Even if an individual has enough knowledge about an innovation and has formed a favorable attitude towards it, adoption is not guaranteed. At this point in the innovation-decision process, research has identified the KAP-gap (cf. chapter 2) that keeps many innovations from being adopted.

3. **Decision:** At the decision stage, the individual takes steps to start using the innovation or abandons it.

4. **Implementation:** The individuals starts using the innovation.

5. *Confirmation:* As long as an individual has adopted an innovation, she will constantly monitor whether it still makes sense to keep doing so — sometimes deciding to abandon the innovation, e.g. if a new innovation appears that can solve the same problems in a more efficient or effective manner.

This thesis' approach supports stages 1 through 4 (printed bold above) and helps mitigating the KAP-gap (2.a). Fig. 7.1 illustrates this relationship.

As chapter 2 has argued, a lack of motivation can increase the likelihood of an individual to stop their adoption after the persuasion stage — in the KAP-gap. The following sections will therefore use knowledge, persuasion, *motivation*, decision, and implementation as the categories for the adoption patterns. This results in a list of patterns for each stage of the innovation-decision process that PAIP supports.

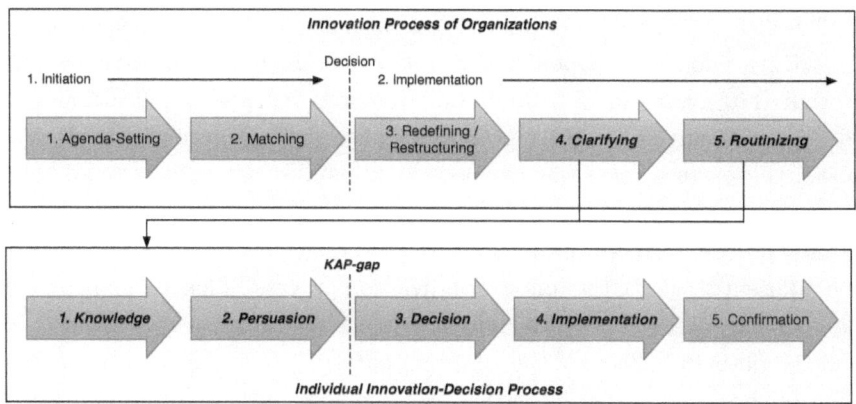

Figure 7.1: *The stages of the innovation process for organizations and the innovation-decision process for individuals. When the organization is in the* Clarifying *or* Routinizing *stages, the individual innovation-decision process becomes relevant. Stages supported by PAIP are printed bold.*

7.1.1. Procedure

The adoption patterns presented later in this chapter were derived from a broad literature review. The goal was to find solutions to adoption problems that can influence individuals in the aforementioned stages of the innovation-decision process without changing the software engineering practice itself (cf. section 1.3). To obtain a list of such solutions, the literature review was conducted across several fields, such as psychology, sociology, software engineering, CSCW, and human-computer interaction. Because of the necessary breadth of this review, conducting a systematic literature review (as e.g. proposed by Kitchenham [92]) was not appropriate.

To find applicable literature, a range of keywords was used during searches in different repositories[1]. The author contacted experts in the respective sub-fields[2] and inquired to them about further applicable literature. In addition, references used by the literature found so far were used to discover more relevant research results. After this process, the list of possibly relevant results consisted of 634 publications.

---

[1]Google Scholar, the ACM Digital Library, IEEE Xplore, and the local university's library.

[2]E.g. social media for software engineering, gamification, or the psychology of motivation.

This list of publications was then scrutinized for their applicability to improving adoption. Open and selective coding (cf. e.g. Strauss and Corbin [170]) were used to find commonalities in these publications and to cluster them into related problems and solution approaches. At this point, the pattern form was decided upon, as abstract cores around solutions became identifiable while the concrete implementations differed.

This process resulted in 54 adoption patterns that were then assigned to the different stages of the innovation-decision process. This assignment was based on the needs of potential adopters in each of the stages (cf. chapter 2) and the potential effects of the adoption patterns. This list of patterns was then further reduced to 24 entries by removing overly specific and overly general ones. Only those adoption patterns were kept that are specific enough to enable a change agent to implement the pattern in a treatment, yet general enough to result in different implementations for each use in an intervention.

Upon finalization of this list of 24 adoption patterns, another keyword search for each pattern was conducted to find more related research results to include in the patterns. This additional information guides change agents in implementing the patterns, and facilitates a more thorough discussion of each pattern's theoretical background.

Finally, properties of adoption patterns were extracted that guide a change agent when deciding for a list of patterns to implement in their specific situation. These properties are used in PAIP's step 3 and are shown in Table 7.1 at the end of this section.

Certain phrasings appear in multiple patterns when discussing similar principles. This repetition is a conscious choice: each pattern should be comprehensible on its own.

7.1.2. Pattern Format

To provide a consistent appearance, each pattern conforms to the following format.

Pattern Name

A pattern's name is a short phrase describing the *solution* the pattern proposes. It is often reduced to an adjective and a noun.

Problem: Which adoption problem does this adoption pattern solve?

Solution: What is the solution to the problem?

Rationale: How and why does this adoption pattern work?

Discussion: How does this adoption pattern fit into larger theories?

Prerequisites: Which prerequisites are necessary to apply this adoption pattern?

Examples: What are successful applications of this adoption pattern? The change agent can use these examples of successful instantiations of the pattern to base their own intervention on.

Related Adoption Patterns: Which other adoption patterns are related to this one, and how?

A consistent format for all adoption patterns improves readability, makes comparisons easier, and helps existing patterns serve as examples for others wishing to propose new patterns.

7.1.3. Limitations

All adoption patterns are based both on established theoretical frameworks as well as peer-reviewed empirical studies and evaluations. Nevertheless, there are several limitations.

- Adoption patterns that were evaluated with individuals that are not software developers, with student developers, or with open source developers might not be transferable to developers in companies.

- Adoption patterns that were evaluated with developers in specific companies might not be transferable to other companies, as company culture can vary widely [6].

- Adoption patterns that were evaluated in public virtual communities might not be transferable to companies. Results may even differ between different virtual communities [114].

- Adoption patterns that were evaluated targeting individuals from a western culture might not be transferable to other cultures. Henrich et al. [85] show that WEIRD societies — "Western, Educated, Industrialized, Rich, and Democratic" — are outliers relative to the entire human race. Yet, most scientific studies investigate subjects from these societies.

The adoption patterns documented in this thesis have been evaluated in one or more situations before, most of them with subjects from individualistic, Western societies. This indicates that they may work similarly in other situations with subjects from similar societies. However, it cannot be guaranteed that the adoption patterns have the expected results in *any* situation. Change agents need to be aware of this fact when evaluating PAIP for use in their own contexts. The iterative nature of PAIP alleviates this shortcoming to a degree, giving change agents an explicit opportunity to fine-tune their interventions to their specific situations.

Finally, I evaluated an early version of PAIP and a subset of the patterns in a student project (cf. chapter 8). Even though more extensive evaluations are desirable in almost any research project, further evaluations of the derived adoption patterns were not possible in the scope of this thesis.

7.1.4. Overview

Table 7.1 provides an overview of all adoption patterns that were derived through the aforementioned process. Apart from the pattern name and the section where it can be found in this thesis, the table shows for which adoption problems a pattern is suitable and which requirements apply.

Some patterns use extrinsic motivators. As will be discussed in the pattern descriptions themselves, these should only be used for *starting* practice adoption or for *intensifying* the use of a *routine* practice. To make this distinction clear in table 7.1, some checkmarks have a corresponding footnote attached[3].

---

[3]Uses extrinsic motivators — use only to *start* creative tasks.

| | | suitable for | | | | requires | |
Pattern	Section	Starting Adoption	Improving Adoption	Creative Tasks	Routine Tasks	Existing Adopters	Meaningful Metric
Knowledge Stage							
Mass Medium	7.2.1	✓	✓	✓	✓		
Microblog	7.2.2	✓	✓	✓	✓	✓	
Voice for Help	7.2.3	✓	✓	✓	✓	✓	
Reputation for Help	7.2.4	✓	✓	✓	✓	✓	✓
Persuasion Stage							
Normative Behavior	7.3.1	✓	✓	✓	✓	✓	
Social Anchor	7.3.2	✓	✓	✓	✓	✓	✓
Peer Recommender	7.3.3	✓	✓	✓	✓	✓	
Motivation: KAP-gap							
Triggers	7.4.1	✓	✓	✓	✓		
Potential Value	7.4.2	✓	✓	✓	✓		✓
Appreciation	7.4.3		✓	✓	✓		
Reputation for Adoption	7.4.4	✓	✓	✓³	✓		✓
Points & Levels	7.4.5	✓	✓	✓³	✓		✓
Leaderboard	7.4.6	✓	✓	✓³	✓		✓
Relative Ranking	7.4.7	✓			✓	✓	✓
Decision Stage							
Challenge	7.5.1	✓	✓	✓	✓		
Embrace Examples	7.5.2	✓	✓	✓	✓		
Incremental Engagement	7.5.3	✓	✓	✓	✓		
Implementation Stage							
Progress Feedback	7.6.1		✓	✓	✓		✓
Performance Feedback	7.6.2		✓	✓	✓		✓
Supporting							
Tuned Activity	7.7.1	✓	✓	✓	✓	✓	
Review	7.7.2	✓	✓	✓	✓		
Meta-Review	7.7.3	✓	✓	✓	✓		
Automatic Badges	7.7.4	✓	✓	✓³	✓		✓
Peer Badges	7.7.5	✓	✓	✓	✓		

Table 7.1.: *An overview of the suitability and requirements for all adoption patterns.*

7.2. Knowledge Stage

This section describes adoption patterns that can support the knowledge stage: the first stage of the innovation-decision process. Developers that are in this stage do not yet have the knowledge necessary to apply the practice. The patterns show how such knowledge can be communicated using interventions.

7.2.1. Mass Medium

Problem: Developers lack awareness or how-to knowledge for a software engineering practice.

Solution: Actively distribute knowledge about the practice to developers.

Rationale: To apply a practice, awareness and how-to knowledge are essential [149]. Actively distributing it is an effective way to inform developers [140].

Discussion: The active distribution of how-to knowledge is an important instrument used by change agents [149]. Mass media, as a channel in Rogers' model of innovation diffusion, are fast and efficient in creating awareness knowledge [149].

Prerequisites: None known.

Examples: In their study of developers on GitHub, Pham et al. [140] report that actively communicating what kinds of tests a project requires helps potential contributors to make more desirable pull requests.

Related Adoption Patterns: Can use a *Microblog* as its channel.

7.2.2. Microblog

Problem: Knowledge about how to apply a software engineering practice does not diffuse sufficiently between developers.

Solution: Let developers connect with each other on an internal microblogging service.

Rationale: Microblogs can improve the diffusion of knowledge inside organizations [147], especially by creating weak links [78] that diffuse knowledge between otherwise isolated communities [32].

Discussion: Interpersonal networks play an important role in persuading individuals to accept new ideas [149] (cf. section 7.3). Beyond that, the presence of weak ties to other communities — e.g. other teams or departments — is important to spread awareness and how-to knowledge further [149, 32].

Prerequisites: Some developers must already have how-to knowledge about the software engineering practice.

Examples: Riemer et al. [147] report on a study on successful enterprise microblogging, finding that it is used for information sharing, mutual help, and coordination.

Related Adoption Patterns: To use the Microblog for the Persuasion stage, consider the *Normative Behavior* pattern.

7.2.3. Voice for Help

Problem: Developers need to learn about the high-level concepts for a practice.

Solution: Provide a space for developers to publish experience reports.

Rationale: High-level concepts — principles knowledge — can support the adoption of a practice [149]. Having accepted peers publish this knowledge can communicate concepts and values to novices [140].

Discussion: Principles knowledge helps understanding how and why an innovation works. While it is possible to adopt an innovation without such knowledge, adoption interventions are more likely to have sustainable effects when individuals have principles knowledge [149]. Because of their influence and large interpersonal networks, opinion leaders are instrumental in diffusing knowledge about an innovation [149].

Prerequisites: Some developers must already be applying the practice.

Examples: Open source developers use blogs to communicate high-level concepts relevant to their development experiences, prompting exchanges with other developers [133].

Related Adoption Patterns: Encourage developers to publish their reports by explicitly giving *Reputation for Help*.

7.2.4. Reputation for Help

Problem: Developers have how-to knowledge that would help other users adopting the practice, but they do not publish it.

Solution: Encourage developers to publish their experiences by explicitly awarding them reputation for doing so.

Rationale: Awarding reputation in the form of explicit points or badges can motivate developers to share their knowledge with peers [48, 116, 111].

Discussion: Reputation is an extrinsic motivator: it is external to the activity to be motivated. Extrinsic motivators have been shown to be hard to sustain over time [44]. However, they can be appropriate for jumpstarting the adoption of a previously unknown practice [149]. Campbell [24] warns that if such measures have real implications — e.g. promotions or changes in salary — their playful nature is removed and the measure is likely to be corrupted (e.g. by manipulation). Sylwester and Roberts [176] show that reputation supports cooperative activities.

114

Prerequisites: Extrinsic rewards like reputation points or badges need to have a meaning that is accepted in the community [99] — in this case, the developer population. Halavais [82] as well as Hamari and Eranti [83] provide guidelines on the effective design of badges.

Examples: Stack Overflow, a question & answer site for developers, uses this pattern very successfully [116].

Related Adoption Patterns: Both *Automatic Badges* and *Peer Badges* suggest strategies for implementing this pattern. *Reputation for Adoption* is a pattern that uses a similar mechanism, but with a different goal.

7.3. Persuasion Stage

Being aware of a practice and knowing how to apply it is not sufficient to adopt it. First, a developer must become willing to try it. This section describes adoption patterns that can support developers in this persuasion stage. Here, the availability of how-to knowledge is an implicit prerequisite for all patterns.

7.3.1. Normative Behavior

Problem: Some developers are using the practice to a satisfactory degree, some are not. The goal is for more developers to start applying the practice or to start applying the practice to a more satisfactory degree.

Solution: Make explicit what normative behavior should be by continuously publishing the behavior of developers, positively emphasizing desirable behavior.

Rationale: Most people wish to act according to social norms and take cues from their environment to find out what is considered normal among their peers. This forms one of the bases of social learning theory [9] and has been confirmed in studies and experiments [22, 64].

Discussion: According to Rogers [149], individuals are more likely to try and adopt an innovation when they can perceive that others — especially opinion leaders — have adopted the innovation. In Rogers' terms, this pattern improves the *observability* of the practice. Visible acceptance of an innovation among one's peers also provides cues regarding its compatibility with one's belief system. Both properties are related to increased adoption of innovations [149].

Prerequisites: The software engineering practice must either produce distinct activities or distinct events must have been derived from the practice if it consists only of continuous activities. This allows activity to be explicitly posted, e.g. on a *Microblog*.

Examples: Chapter 8 reports on a quasi-experiment in which we used a newsfeed displaying commit messages. Commits with messages appeared normal, while commits without messages displayed *"No commit message given"* in red. In the experiment, students were more likely to enter commit messages than the control group. Sukumaran et al. [173] show that the behavior of commenters on web sites can determine the behavior of subsequent commenters.

Related Adoption Patterns: A *Social Anchor* uses a similar mechanism, but works with aggregated behavior. *Triggers* can direct developers' attention on normative behavior. *Tuned Activity* moderates the amount of updates a developer receives.

7.3.2. Social Anchor

Problem: Some developers are using the software engineering practice to a satisfactory degree, some are not. More developers should start using the practice.

Solution: Display an aggregated measurement to developers that represents the degree of compliance with a software engineering practice. State that this measurement is the value recorded for the developer's peers and ensure that it is a desirable value. Compare this value with the developer's own value. Add a value judgement containing approval or disapproval of the developer's performance with regard to her peers.

Rationale: Most people wish to act according to social norms and take cues from their environment to find out what is considered normal among their peers. This forms one of the bases of social learning theory [9] and has been confirmed in several studies and experiments [154, 14]. Schultz et al. [158] find that messages of social approval and disapproval can improve compliance for non-compliers and can keep it stable for those already complying.

Discussion: Individuals are more likely to try and adopt an innovation when they can perceive that others have adopted the innovation [149]. Visible acceptance of an innovation among one's peers provides cues regarding its compatibility with one's belief system. Both properties are related to increased adoption of innovations [149].

Prerequisites: It must be possible to express a desirable aspect of the software engineering practice as an aggregation (e.g. test coverage for improving the adoption of unit testing). Some developers must already be applying the metric in desirable quality.

Examples: Salganik et al. [154, 155] report on experimental studies in which they manipulate the perceived popularity of music by displaying download counts for songs. The authors find that popularity determines success, while the actual quality of the music has a lesser influence.

Related Adoption Patterns: This pattern is related to *Normative Behavior*: it uses similar mechanisms, but displays behavior in aggregation.

7.3.3. Peer Recommender

Problem: Developers with low proficiency in a practice are not sufficiently exposed to developers with high proficiency in the practice.

Solution: Recommend similar and more proficient peers to less proficient developers.

Rationale: Individuals that are perceived to be similar to a person are more persuasive than others [62]. Ties with others can support and influence individuals in adopting an innovation [149]. Similar, yet more proficient developers should thus be able to positively influence another developer with regard to their adoption of a practice.

Discussion: Authorative figures, such as experts and opinion leaders, can support the diffusion of an innovation with their heightened influence over their peers [149]. Accordingly, suggesting such ties can support the adoption of a practice.

Prerequisites: Developers more proficient in the practice than the targeted developers must be available.

Examples: Guzzi and Begel [81] report on their *CARES* tool, which helps developers to find experts on a certain piece of source code. Damian et al. [40] discuss *Requirements-centric Social Networks* that can help finding experts in requirements engineering tasks.

Related Adoption Patterns: This pattern can be combined with *Microblog* or *Normative Behavior* by suggesting connections between developers. Used alone, it can e.g. suggest experts on specific artefacts as demonstrated by Guzzi and Begel [81].

7.4. Motivation: Overcoming the KAP-gap

Even when they are able to apply a practice and have a favorable attitude towards it, some individuals will not adopt it — this is called the KAP-gap [149]. As chapter 2 has argued, motivation can play a role in this process. This section describes adoption patterns that can support the motivation of developers for overcoming the KAP-gap.

7.4.1. Triggers

Problem: Developers are able to apply a practice, but do not do so at all or not frequently enough.

Solution: Use notifications to cue developers to applying a practice by directing their attention to a task related to the practice. To support motivation, associate triggers with positive feedback or a goal to be reached. Do not overload developers with triggers.

Rationale: According to Fogg's behavior model [63], ability and motivation are not enough to enact a behavior — in addition, a trigger is needed. Positive feedback that is informational rather than controlling [44] as well as clear, challenging goals [108] both support motivation. Dynamically adjusting notifications can avoid information overload [190]. The effect may wear off relatively quickly [2].

Discussion: Fogg [63] distinguishes three kinds of triggers: those supporting motivation, those improving perceived ability, and pure reminders. While reminders are important in software development to lower the cognitive load [135], this pattern suggests using motivational triggers so that only ability is a prerequisite. Rogers agrees that such a *cue-to-action* can serve to close the KAP-gap [149].

Prerequisites: Developers already have the ability to apply the software engineering practice.

Examples: Abdolrasulnia et al. [2] used email reminders to trigger desired behavior in physicians.

Related Adoption Patterns: This pattern can support many other patterns by making their implementation more salient. E.g., *Triggers* can be used to remind developers of a *Challenge* or to notify them of an *Appreciation*.

7.4.2. Potential Value

Problem: Developers cannot see the value in a practice. This decreases frequency or quality of their application of the practice.

Solution: Provide developers with feedback on the value their application of the practice could produce for others.

Rationale: Individuals are motivated by meaningful work. Having a positive impact on others supports perceiving a task as meaningful [6].

Discussion: Individuals are reluctant to adopt preventive innovations — those that promise to avert an undesirable future event —, as their value is not immediately visible or might never materialize. Therefore, the KAP-gap is often found for preventive innovations [149]. Many software engineering practices are preventive: e.g., documentation is supposed to support future maintenance, and decoupling systems is supposed to make future integrations easier. Lavallée and Robillard [102] report that the absence of value feedback in many requirements of software process improvement (SPI) initiatives can be detrimental to developer motivation, as the process changes create no directly perceivable improvements. This is related to the fact that SPI only becomes valuable after some time [102]. Therefore, when providing value feedback, rough estimates might be preferable to no value feedback at all (cf. Rashid et al. [143]).

Prerequisites: The value of a contribution must be estimable for the software engineering practice.

Examples: In a study on experience sampling, Hsieh et al. [86] show that feedback on the value of an individual's efforts can increase contributions. Rashid et al. [143] show similar effects for an online community, differentiating several alternative designs for estimating value.

Related Adoption Patterns: Depending on the adoption problem, a different kind of feedback may be more suitable. *Progress Feedback* and *Performance Feedback* provide alternatives.

7.4.3. Appreciation

Problem: Developers have adopted a practice to a degree, but its application is not intensive or frequent enough.

Solution: Enable developers to appreciate each other's work in a visible and persistent manner.

Rationale: Concrete and sincere appreciation from peers can improve an individual's motivation with regard to a task [6]. Automatic appreciation — messages generated by a computer program — do not mean as much as that given by a human being [122].

Discussion: This pattern should support the motivational needs of competence and relatedness and would therefore lead to higher motivation with regard to the practice [44].

Prerequisites: There must be consumers of the results of applying the practice who will have a reason to appreciate these results.

Examples: On the developer profile aggregator Coderwall, developers can endorse each other. In a study by Singer et al. [162], developers reported enjoying this recognition of their development skills by others. Cheshire and Antin [28] manipulated a banner on a website to thank users, resulting in more contributions from these users.

Related Adoption Patterns: *Triggers* can be used to notify developers of appreciation, directing their attention to this positive feedback.

7.4.4. Reputation for Adoption

Problem: Developers are not applying the practice at all or not frequently enough.

Solution: Encourage developers to apply the practice by explicitly awarding them reputation for doing so.

Rationale: Awarding reputation in the form of explicit points or badges can motivate developers to try out a practice or to apply it more often [162, 48, 116].

Discussion: Reputation is an extrinsic motivator: it is external to the activity to be motivated. Extrinsic motivators have been shown to be hard to sustain over time [44]. However, they can be appropriate for jumpstarting the adoption of a previously unknown practice [149]. Alternatively, this pattern can be used to motivate routine activities — for these, extrinsic motivators do not interfere with intrinsic motivators [44]. Campbell [24] warns that if such measures have real implications — e.g. promotions or changes in salary — their playful nature is removed and the measure is likely to be corrupted (e.g. by manipulation). Sylwester and Roberts [176] show that reputation supports cooperative activities.

Prerequisites: Extrinsic rewards like reputation points or badges need to have a meaning that is accepted in the community [99] — in this case, the developer population. Halavais [82] as well as Hamari and Eranti [83] provide guidelines on the effective design of badges.

Examples: According to Casalo et al., reputation is an important motivator in open source development [25].

Related Adoption Patterns: Both *Automatic Badges* and *Peer Badges* suggest strategies for implementing this pattern. *Reputation for Help* is a pattern that uses a similar mechanism, but with a different goal.

7.4.5. Points & Levels

Problem: Developers have not yet started applying the practice or a routine activity that is already being applied should be intensified.

Solution: Award points and levels for the activity that is to be started or intensified. Provide a space for users to display their points and levels, e.g. on a user profile. Give clear instructions on how to attain different levels.

Rationale: Extrinsic motivators — even intangible ones like points or levels — are appropriate for jumpstarting a new behavior and for motivating routine work [44]. The public display of points and levels can make developers feel proud for their achievements [162]. Transparent goals are more likely to motivate individuals [108].

Discussion: Points and Levels are very extrinsic motivators — that is, individuals will carry out the activity not for its own sake, but to obtain a reward. Extrinsic motivators have been shown to be hard to sustain over time [44]. However, they can be appropriate for jumpstarting the adoption of a previously unknown practice [149]. Alternatively, this pattern can be used to motivate routine activities — for these, extrinsic motivators do not interfere with intrinsic motivaton [44]. Yet, in all cases it is important to only reward activities that should really be intensified, and in exactly the desired quality. Otherwise, e.g. if only quantitiy is rewarded, quality can suffer — as it would not be instrumental in obtaining the reward (cf. Thom et al. [178]). Campbell [24] warns that if such measures have real implications — e.g. promotions or changes in salary — their playful nature is removed and the measure is likely to be corrupted (e.g. by manipulation).

Prerequisites: A metric that quantifies the activity that is to be motivated. Ideally, the metric cannot be manipulated by developers who wish to gain more points.

Examples: Farzan et al. [58] report on an enterprise social network site in which points and levels were awarded for posting comments and other activities. This intervention increased activity. Thom et al. [178] later report on the removal of these mechanisms from the site, resulting in a significant decrease in activity — especially regarding nonsense comments. Montola et al. [123] added an achievement system to a photo sharing site, resulting in friendly competition, yet also some concerns from users who believed that the achievements might motivate undesirable behavior.

Related Adoption Patterns: Based on *Points & Levels*, a *Leaderboard* can be used to rank developers against each other, creating an explicit competitive situation.

7.4.6. Leaderboard

Problem: Developers have not yet started applying the practice or a routine activity that is already being applied should be intensified.

Solution: Use a metric that measures compliance with the software engineering practice to rank developers against each other, creating explicit competition. If possible, let groups compete against each other instead of individual developers against each other.

Rationale: For some populations, competition is a strong motivator, leading to improved performance and higher perseverance [177]. Group affiliation positively influences achievement motivation [189].

Discussion: Competition can be an effective motivator for populations that are interested in challenges, strive to increase their own competence, and strive to outperform others [177]. Winning increases motivation by increasing perceived competence [144]. However, a pressured context can decrease motivation by diminishing perceived self-determination [144]. As reported by Deci et al. [45], for populations without the above characteristics, competition can also decrease motivation. As losing at least has no positive effects on motivation [144], groups of developers should be ranked in separate lists that match their respective competence levels [117, 89].

Prerequisites: A metric that quantifies the activity that is to be motivated. Ideally, the metric cannot be manipulated by developers who wish to improve their ranking. To obtain desirable results, the developer population must have competitive characteristics and the competition context must not be controlling (cf. *Discussion*).

Examples: Chapter 8 reports on a quasi-experiment in which we used a Leaderboard to rank students according to their number of commits to version control. Students in the treatment group committed significantly more often than those from the control group. According to the German airline pilots association *Vereinigung Cockpit e.V.*, the airline *Ryanair* uses a leaderboard to rank pilots by their kerosene savings [187]. As this was used to coerce pilots into using less fuel, pilots reported feeling psychological pressure and risking emergency landings [187]. This illustrates that a controlling or pressuring competitive context can lead to dysfunctional results.

Related Adoption Patterns: *Points & Levels* can be used as the metric to rank developers.

124

7.4.7. Relative Ranking

Problem: Developers have not yet started applying the practice or a routine activity that is already being applied should be intensified.

Solution: Use a metric that measures compliance with the software engineering practice to rank developers against each other. Only show individual developers their relative ranking as compared to all other developers, creating an anonymous form of competition.

Rationale: For some populations, competition is a strong motivator, leading to improved performance and higher perseverance [177]. However, open competition can have several undesirable side effects (cf. *Leaderboard* adoption pattern). Competing against an aggregated, anonymous metric (*"you are in the top 5%"*) can eliminate some of these drawbacks.

Discussion: Competition can be an effective motivator for populations that are interested in challenges, strive to increase their own competence, and strive to outperform others [177]. Open competition can have several drawbacks, however. As Wilson and Sell [193] show, too much information about others' past behavior can be detrimental to contribution levels. Cheshire and Antin [28] show that relative rankings do not suffer from these effects. Also cf. with the *Discussion* of the *Leaderboard* adoption pattern.

Prerequisites: A metric that quantifies the activity that is to be motivated. Ideally, the metric cannot be manipulated by developers who wish to improve their ranking. To obtain desirable results, the developer population must have competitive characteristics and the competition context must not be controlling (cf. *Discussion*).

Examples: Cheshire and Antin [28] report on an experiment in which relative ranking was successfully used to increase contributions from members of an online community.

Related Adoption Patterns: Compared to the *Leaderboard* pattern, a *Relative Ranking* removes some of the potentially damaging side effects of open competition. Similar to the *Social Anchor*, information about others' behavior is presented in an aggregated form. However, the *Relative Ranking* frames the interaction as competitive, whereas the *Social Anchor* has a normative framing.

7.5. Decision Stage

In the decision stage, developers know about the practice, have a favorable attitude towards it, and are motivated to apply it. To further reduce uncertainty, they will now try the practice, possibly on a probationary basis. The adoption patterns in this category support them in this stage.

7.5.1. Challenge

Problem: Developers are not improving their adoption of a software engineering practice.

Solution: Provide developers with explicit, attainable, and challenging goals. Make sure developers understand what the conditions for attaining the goal are and give explicit feedback on results. Prefer challenges that require the developer to learn something new over those that merely require reaching a certain performance as measured by a metric.

Rationale: Providing individuals with clear and challenging, yet attainable goals can prompt them to reach these goals and increases their performance with regard to the goals [108]. Learning goals are more effective than performance goals [113, 53].

Discussion: In the persuasion stage, individuals need to be prompted to try out an innovation [149]. Goal-setting can provide this prompt. Clear feedback and a sense of achievement have a positive influence on motivation [108] and will thus help individuals avoiding the KAP-gap.

Prerequisites: A set of goals with the above qualities must be available or be derived for the software engineering practice.

Examples: Zhu et al. [197] show that goal-setting improves the performance of editors on Wikipedia. In studies of two manipulated collaboration systems, Jung et al. [88] demonstrate that clear goals and feedback can enhance performance. Ling et al. [107] manipulated an online movie recommender website and found that specific and challenging goals prompted individuals to contribute.

Related Adoption Patterns: Support this pattern by giving developers *Progress Feedback*. *Automatic Badges* or *Peer Badges* can act as symbols for completing a *Challenge*.

7.5.2. Embrace Examples

Problem: Developers are not using a practice because they do not know how to begin, or they are applying the practice in an incorrect or deficient manner.

Solution: Display examples prominently and make them easily accessible and customizable. Explain how they work and why they are good examples. Emphasize that using examples is desired.

Rationale: Developers learn best practices from existing examples and customize them for their needs [140]. Explanations help in understanding the examples and may support the application of the contained principles in future tasks [127]. Since developers may disregard example usage as a bad practice [10, 75], they need to be an officially accepted practice in development and may at times be preferable to other alternatives [75].

Discussion: Examples increase the perceived trialability of a software engineering practice [140]. Trialability is positively correlated with adoption [149].

Prerequisites: Examples for how the practice is to be applied must be available.

Examples: Projects on GitHub can support new contributors by having a clearly named folder for tests. Users of GitHub report that they use those existing tests as examples and customize them to write their own tests [140]. Answers on the question & answer site Stack Overflow often contain examples. These are most useful when they contain an explanation [127].

Related Adoption Patterns: Examples and their use can be promoted using the *Microblog* and *Voice for Help* adoption patterns.

7.5.3. Incremental Engagement

Problem: Developers do not apply the practice at all, or do not apply it as frequently or intensively as desired.

Solution: Tailor the available tasks to the current level of a developer's proficiency. Suggest these tailored tasks to the developer.

Rationale: Individuals are motivated most by tasks that match or slightly exceed their current abilities [108]. Directing an individual's attention to behavior that they are motivated to enact and that matches their abilities can support them in actually adopting the behavior [63]. Kim [91] as well as Preece and Shneiderman [141] show how segmenting online communities into five respectively four classes and subsequently tailoring tasks can improve contributions and engagement.

Discussion: Because of their personality traits and abilities, individuals in different adopter categories (innovators, early adopters, etc.) will respond to different kinds of motivators [149]. Personalizing the adoption process supports developers of different proficiency levels in adopting a practice.

Prerequisites: A segmentation of the developer population that consists of developer groups with distinct proficiency levels and support requirements. This segmentation then guides the creation of tailored tasks to be suggested to the members of the respective groups.

Examples: López et al. [110] successfully used this pattern in an online community for academic conferences, increasing contributions by its members.

Related Adoption Patterns: This pattern is a combination of the *Challenge* and *Triggers* patterns. In addition, it employs a personalization strategy to match the different segments of the developer population.

7.6. Implementation Stage

The adoption patterns in this category support software developers in the implementation stage. In this stage, developers are starting to put the software engineering practice to use in their daily work. The following patterns further reduce any uncertainty about whether an individual is applying the practice correctly by giving different kinds of feedback.

7.6.1. Progress Feedback

Problem: The frequency or persistence of developers' application of a practice are not satisfactory.

Solution: Provide developers with positive feedback on the progress they are making in their application of the practice.

Rationale: Feedback on progress can motivate individuals to reach a goal [108].

Discussion: Feedback on progress enables individuals to adjust their efforts and strategies to reach a goal faster or more efficiently [108]. Artificially increasing the perceived progress can lead to greater persistance, increases the likelihood of completing the task, and decreases the time required for task completion [129, 93]. Sach and Petre [152] document a study suggesting that positive feedback has positive effects on software engineers' job satisfaction, while negative feedback impacts behavior. This is supported by Amabile and Kramer [6], who show that positive feedback can not only lead to higher job satisfaction, but also to better performance on creative tasks. When applied to a learning goal as is often required in software development, feedback on progress can have a positive effect on reaching that goal [186, 53].

Prerequisites: Progress must be measurable for the software engineering practice, i.e., a metric must supply the current progress and the a value for which completion is defined.

Examples: Niebuhr and Kerkow [128] demonstrate that feedback on progress can motivate users of a computer system for repetitive tasks. Schunk and Swartz [159] show that feedback on progress can increase performance even for more creative tasks, such as writing.

Related Adoption Patterns: Depending on the adoption problem, a different kind of feedback may be more suitable. *Performance Feedback* and *Potential Value* provide alternatives.

7.6.2. Performance Feedback

Problem: Frequency or quality of developers' application of the practice are not satisfactory.

Solution: Provide developers with feedback on their performance regarding their application of the practice, compared with their own past performance.

Rationale: Feedback on performance can enable and motivate individuals to improve their performance [5, 108].

Discussion: Feedback on performance is widely and successfully used to improve employee performance [5]. However, software development as a profession requires employees to constantly learn and develop themselves. Dweck [53] summarizes several studies that show that for learning contexts, focusing on performance goals can be significantly less effective than learning goals (cf. also Lunenburg [113]). Thus, for adoption problems that require developers to learn new material, the *Progress Feedback* pattern is more appropriate.

Prerequisites: Performance must be measurable for the software engineering practice.

Examples: Jung et al. [88] show that performance feedback integrated into an idea generation tool can improve individuals' performance.

Related Adoption Patterns: This pattern is similar to *Leaderboard* and *Relative Ranking*, in that it enables competition with oneself. Depending on the adoption problem, a different kind of feedback may be more suitable. *Progress Feedback* and *Potential Value* provide alternatives.

7.7. Supporting Adoption Patterns

The following patterns cannot be implemented on their own, but require one or more of the aforementioned adoption patterns to be in use. They provide solutions to some problems that can be encountered with interventions using those patterns.

7.7.1. Tuned Activity

Problem: Participation in interventions is low, reducing their effect.

Solution: Tune the visible activity levels of the intervention so that there is enough activity to make participants feel part of a lively community, but do not overload them. If necessary, generate artificial activity.

Rationale: The appearance of a lively community through visible activity increases participation [131, 37], but too much activity can lead to information overload [40, 190, 42].

Discussion: Rogers reports that a determining factor for the successful adoption of many innovations is critical mass [149]. Potential adopters are aware of this phenomenon and adjust their adoption behavior accordingly: if an innovation is perceived as having reached critical mass, adoption increases [149].

Prerequisites: An intervention or another system emitting activity information must be in use or planned to be used.

Examples: The social media site reddit[4] used fake accounts to appear lively and stimulate community formation[5]. Wang et al. [190] developed a dynamic awareness system that improved the perceived utility of the system for its users by reducing unwanted activity.

Related Adoption Patterns: This pattern can support a *Microblog*, *Normative Behavior*, and *Triggers*.

7.7.2. Review

Problem: An adoption pattern requires a metric, but no acceptable one is available.

Solution: Let developers provide reviews of others' contributions and use review scores as a surrogate metric.

Rationale: Several adoption patterns require a metric to quantitatively measure compliance to provide feedback, award badges, or compare performance. Many of the known software engineering metrics are not acceptable for these patterns, as they require interpretation in context. Reviews by developers alleviate this problem by adding an interpretation step by a human.

Discussion: Metrics in software engineering are prone to misinterpretation if not interpreted in context [18]. Reviews are an accepted alternative to measure qualities for which no automatic metric is available — e.g. in software engineering [148] and academia [165].

Prerequisites: Developers must be motivated to conduct reviews. As reviews can be seen as simply another software engineering practice for which adoption must be improved, adoption patterns can be used to mitigate this problem.

---

[4]http://reddit.com
[5]According to an interview with reddit founder Alexis Ohanian: http://bigthink.com/ideas/23998

Examples: Code reviews are an accepted practice in software engineering, in industry as well as open source [148]. The news website Slashdot[6] successfully uses reviews to moderate the quality of comments on news articles [98].

Related Adoption Patterns: The *Meta-Review* can improve the quality of the metric resulting from the reviews.

7.7.3. Meta-Review

Problem: The quality of reviews gained through the Review pattern is unsatisfactory.

Solution: Let other developers review the reviews.

Rationale: Having different developers assign a review score to a review itself helps evening out mistakes made by the original reviewers.

Discussion: Consciously or unconsciously malicious developers can endanger the quality of the system established by the *Review* pattern, e.g. by giving consistently low review scores to gain relative advantages themselves. Adding another level of reviews is a common practice to alleviate this problem, e.g. in scholary reviews.

Prerequisites: Developers must be motivated to conduct meta-reviews. As they can be seen as simply another software engineering practice for which adoption must be improved, adoption patterns can be used to mitigate this problem.

Examples: The news website Slashdot[7] successfully uses meta-reviews to moderate the quality of the reviews of comments on news articles [98].

Related Adoption Patterns: This pattern can support the *Review* pattern.

---

[6]http://slashdot.org
[7]http://slashdot.org

7.7.4. Automatic Badges

Problem: A pattern requires that reputation or achievements be made explicit.

Solution: Award meaningful badges of different categories based on explicit, automatic rules.

Rationale: If awarded badges have an accepted meaning in a community, they are more likely to be effective in motivating individuals [99]. Explicit rules make the goal an individual has to reach transparent, supporting motivation [108]. Separating rewards into categories can increase motivation [194].

Discussion: In both competiton and cooperation, individuals rely on signals to assess each other: their experience, reputation, skills, or group affiliations. Social transparency that makes such qualities explicit can support this process [162]. Badges specifically fulfil multiple roles: they can be used for assessment, but also serve as status symbols, assist individuals in setting goals, and can support group identification [7]. Halavais [82] as well as Hamari and Eranti [83] provide guidelines on the effective design of badges.

Prerequisites: An accepted metric must be available that can be used to implement the automatic rules.

Examples: The developer profile aggregator Coderwall[8] awards achievement badges based on an individual's commits to different version control repositories. In a study by Singer et al. [162], developers report that this mechanism motivates them to try out new programming languages.

Related Adoption Patterns: *Peer Badges* are an alternative if no suitable metric for awarding badges is available.

---

[8]http://coderwall.com

7.7.5. Peer Badges

Problem: A pattern requires that reputation or achievements be made explicit, but no suitable metric is available.

Solution: Let developers award badges of different categories to peers based on documented and accepted criteria.

Rationale: If awarded badges have an accepted meaning in a community, they are more likely to be effective in motivating individuals [99]. Informal peer rewards have been shown to increase individual effort [145]. Documented criteria make the goal an individual has to reach transparent, supporting motivation [108]. Separating rewards into categories can increase motivation [194].

Discussion: In both competiton and cooperation, individuals rely on signals to assess each other: their experience, reputation, skills, or group affiliations. Social transparency that makes such qualities explicit can support this process [162]. Badges specifically fulfil multiple roles: they can be used for assessment, but also serve as status symbols, assist individuals in setting goals, and can support group identification [7]. Halavais [82] as well as Hamari and Eranti [83] provide guidelines on the effective design of badges.

Prerequisites: A set of criteria for awarding badges that is accepted by the developer population must be available.

Examples: Wikipedia editors can award *barnstar* badges to fellow contributors. Restivo and van de Rijt show that receiving a *barnstar* can significantly increase effort [145].

Related Adoption Patterns: If a metric is available that is accepted in the developer population, *Automatic Badges* can be used instead.

7.8. Summary

This chapter introduced a catalog of adoption patterns. A change agent applying PAIP can use these patterns to improve the adoption of a software engineering practice in a given situation. The adoption patterns are categorized by the stages in the innovation-decision process they address, with five adoption patterns supporting other patterns. Fig. 7.2 provides an overview of all proposed adoption patterns.

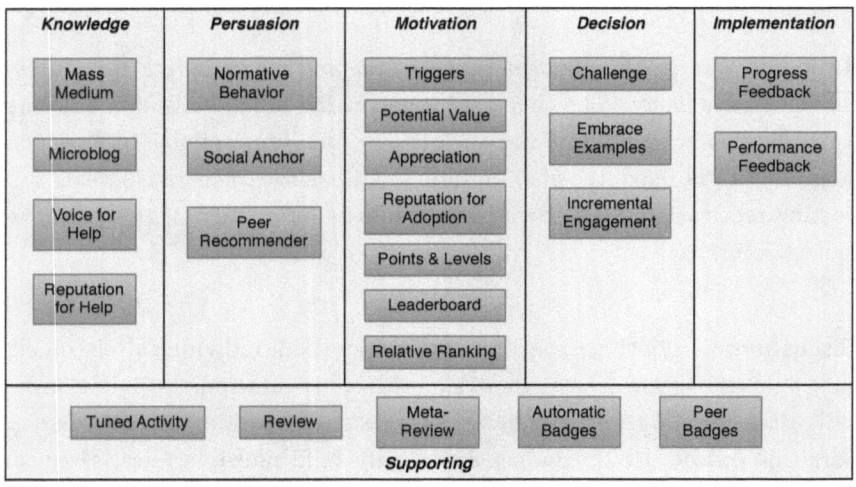

Figure 7.2: *An overview of all adoption patterns and their categories.*

In the **knowledge stage**, diffusing awareness knowledge, how-to knowledge, and principles knowledge about an innovation are important [149]. The *Mass Medium* pattern proposes the simplest approach: distributing knowledge about a practice directly to developers. The *Microblog* supports knowledge diffusion between developers directly. To emphasize the role of opinion leaders, the *Voice for Help* pattern adds a facility for developers to diffuse their own knowledge themselves in a more extensive format, e.g. via company-internal blogs. To support this, the *Reputation for Help* pattern provides an incentive.

During the **persuasion stage**, individuals form an opinion of an innovation [149]. To influence this process, the *Normative Behavior* and *Social Anchor* patterns use effects related to social learning theory [9]. The *Peer*

Recommender pattern supports such processes by suggesting similar or relevant developers to each other.

The **KAP-gap** — a situation in which knowledge and a favorable attitude do not result in adoption — can result from a lack of motivation, the absence of *cues-to-action*, or the preventive nature of an innovation [149]. *Triggers* provide cues to developers to start using a practice. Both *Appreciation* and *Potential Value* can show a developer that a decision to adopt a practice would be beneficial for others, creating meaning. Finally, the extrinsic motivators of the *Reputation for Adoption, Points & Levels, Leaderboard,* and *Relative Ranking* patterns can support developers in trying a new practice and in applying a routine practice more often or intensively.

At the **decision stage**, it is helpful for a potential adopter to try the innovation on a probationary basis. Using research into goal-setting, the *Challenge* pattern suggests tasks related to a practice to developers. The *Embrace Examples* pattern makes an existing practice explicit: the use of examples in software development. While often devalued as "copy and paste coding" [10], it can serve as a powerful device to get developers started with using a practice [140]. The *Incremental Engagement* pattern acknowledges that different developers might be at different proficiency levels and suggests tasks especially tailored to a developer's situation.

In the **implementation stage**, adopters are trying to reduce any remaining uncertainty with regard to the innovation [149]. Both the *Progress Feedback* and the *Performance Feedback* pattern help developers understand whether they applying the practice correctly and how proficient they already are.

This list of adoption patterns is necessarily only a snapshot of what is currently known. New results from research as well as changes in society will make it necessary to revise existing patterns, remove existing ones, or add new ones. Society is not only influenced by technology, but it also shapes technology itself — creating a feedback loop [115]. In this way, the patterns themselves might as well influence their own future evolution.

To show that the combination of PAIP and the adoption pattern catalog can indeed be used to improve the adoption of software engineering practice, the next chapter provides an evaluation of an early version of PAIP and a subset of the adoption patterns in a student project.

8. Quasi-Experiment: Version Control Practices in a Student Project

Together with Stapel and Schneider, I conducted the following quasi-experiment to evaluate whether the process prescribed by PAIP and the associated adoption patterns can be effectively used to improve the adoption of software engineering practices. In a student project lasting a full semester, we attempted to improve the adoption of version control practices in small teams of student developers. We used early versions of both PAIP and the catalog of adoption patterns and used the experience from this evaluation to refine both.

A quasi-experiment is an experiment in which the assignment of subjects to the control vs. treatment conditions is non-random. In our case, the control group was comprised of data from the version control repositories of previous years in which our group organized this project. The treatment group was the cohort of students taking the project in the fall term of 2011. Organization and tasks in all years have been relatively similar.

8.1. Introduction

As has been shown in chapter 5, developers do not always strictly follow software development processes and software engineering practices. Even though individuals may be aware of a practice and its advantages, as well as capable of implementing it, they do not always adopt it — a situation called the KAP-gap (cf. chapter 2).

In centralized version control systems such as Subversion[1], developers should commit early and often to decouple changes from each other and to spot conflicts with the work of other developers earlier [21]. To make browsing historical data easier, each change should include a description of its contents. Even though many developers know of these or similar guidelines, they do not always follow them. This can influence the maintainability — and therefore quality and costs — of a software project negatively.

---

[1]http://subversion.apache.org

Fig. 8.1 shows a commit to a repository hosted on the GitHub social coding website[2]. As he did not commit frequently enough, the author is unable to tell which changes the commit contains. Instead of making several commits and describing them appropriately, he commits all his changes at once with a commit message that does not give a useful description of the contained changes. In a team of software developers, such a commit would be problematic for other team members to comprehend.

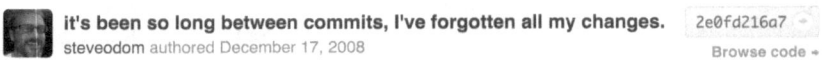

Figure 8.1: *A commit on GitHub.*

We often find similar commits in student projects: developers include several different features and fixes in single commits and leave commit messages empty. This problem occurs regularly, even though the organizers of that student project emphasize each year that they want students to commit regularly, since the version control repository is the only way for our group to continue work on the students' projects later — for which a meaningful commit history would be useful. The organizers also emphasize that other students — peers of the student developers — might need to access the repository in the future, e.g. to improve on one of the student projects for a thesis.

However, the problem persists. We suspect the reason to be a combination of missing knowledge regarding best practices and a lack of motivation for spending the additional effort needed for thoughtful commits. We therefore decided to apply an early version of PAIP in the fall 2011 term's project and used a selection of adoption patterns to create a persuasive intervention to alleviate this problem. Before documenting our application of PAIP, the following section introduces the experiment context.

8.1.1. The Software Project Course

Each fall semester, our research group organizes the *software project* (SWP) course, a mandatory course for computer science undergraduates. The course has roughly 35 to 70 participants every time, most of them in their

---

[2]Source: `https://github.com/steveodom/beta-signup/commits/master/views`, accessed Feb 9th 2012

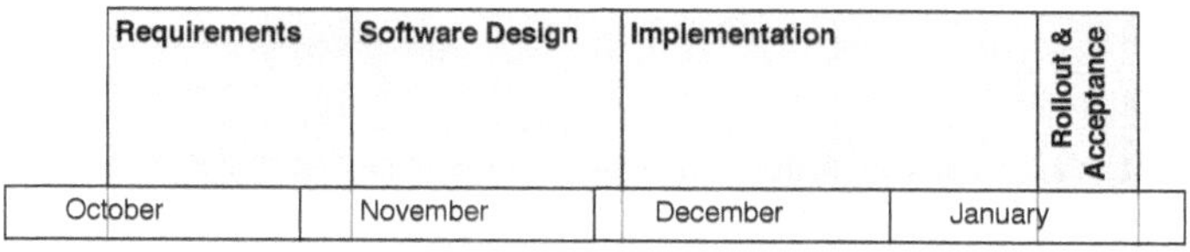

Requirements	Software Design	Implementation	Rollout & Acceptance
October	November	December	January

Figure 8.2: *The process of the software project course.*

fifth semester. The students form teams of four to six members, and elect a project leader as well as a quality agent. The project starts at the beginning of October and lasts until the end of January.

The members of our group act as customers, proposing software projects that we would like to have developed. That way, we are able to provide projects with real requirements while keeping control of their size and technological demands. This is beneficial for the comparability of projects in experiments such as the one presented here. Usually, each student team will work on a different project with a different customer, however some projects may be given to multiple teams to work on independently.

Each project is divided into three main phases: requirements elicitation, software design, and implementation. After that, customers get to try out the produced software and assess their compliance with requirements in a short acceptance phase (cf. Fig. 8.2).

After each phase, the teams have to pass a quality gate (QG) to proceed to the next phase. This ensures a minimum quality of the artifacts developed in each phase. If a team fails a quality gate, they are allowed to refine their artifacts once. Failing the quality gate for a single phase repeatedly would lead to failing the course. However, this has not happened yet.

So far, we have conducted this course every year since 2004. However, for this experiment, we only consider the years starting with 2007, as this was the first year we had the students use Subversion for version control. The process we use and the size of the projects have not changed significantly since then. The duration has constantly been the whole fall semester. While each project is different, we take care to always provide projects with similar requirements regarding effort and proficiency in software development. This is to ensure fairness between the teams with the added benefit of better comparability.

The preconditions regarding the participants have been very stable. Our group teaches all the basic courses on software engineering, software quality, and version control. The contents of these courses have remained similar over the years.

In the first phase, students make appointments with their customers and interview them about their requirements. They produce a requirements specification that they need to get signed by their respective customer to proceed to the next phase. In the second phase, the teams can choose between preparing an architecture or creating exploratory prototypes. In both variants, they are required to produce a software design document. They implement the actual applications in the third and final phase.

During the project, a member of our group will act as coach, answering questions about technical subjects and the development process. To create time scarcity, each team receives six vouchers for customer appointments of 15 minutes each and six vouchers for coach appointments of 30 minutes each.

At the end of the project, the customer executes the acceptance tests from the requirements specification and decides whether rework is needed. Once the customer has finally accepted or rejected the software product, the role-play ends.

Finally, we conduct an *LID* session with each team. LID — short for *Light-weight Documentation of Experiences* — is a technique for the elicitation of project experiences [156]. A typical LID session for the course takes about two hours during which the team members and a moderator jointly fill in a template for experience elicitation. An LID session inquires students about impressions, feelings, conflicts, and advice, and has them review the whole project from beginning to end. In the sessions, we emphasize that their passing of the course will not be affected anymore and encourage them to honestly describe the negative experiences as well.

For each team, we provide a Subversion repository, a Trac[3] instance for issue tracking, and a web-based quality gate system that is used to progress the teams through the project phases. The Trac instance is linked to the team's version control repository, so students are able to see their team's commits using either Trac or any Subversion client.

---

[3]http://trac.edgewall.org

8.2. An Application of PAIP

This section documents how we applied PAIP and deployed a persuasive intervention — with a Web application called *Teamfeed* as its treatment — to a student population of 37 participants. The section's organization is based on PAIP's first five steps: *Characterize Context, Define Adoption Goal & Metrics, Choose Adoption Patterns, Design Treatment*, and *Deploy Intervention*. The succeeding section implements the sixth step: *Analyze Results*.

8.2.1. Characterize Context

In the first step of PAIP, the change agent determines the current context in which PAIP is to be applied. This entails the practice for which adoption should be improved and its properties, as well as the characteristics of the developer population.

The Software Engineering Practice To apply PAIP, the change agent decides whether the practice for which adoption is to be influenced is comprised of primarily routine or creative tasks. This experiment is concerned with practices for committing to version control, which involves deciding when to commit, what to commit, and how to describe it in the commit message. Based on the rough guidelines given in PAIP's description (chapter 6), we determine that our practice entails *creative* tasks.

The Developer Population Regarding the developer population, the change agent determines whether there are any existing adopters of the practice that could act as role models. As we have seen *some* student developers adhering to good committing practices in previous years, we decide that we can indeed assume existing adopters in our population.

8.2.2. Define Adoption Goal & Metrics

In this second step, we define the adoption goal that the intervention should be optimized for. To measure success in the last step, we define metrics.

Defining a Goal As advised by PAIP, we first choose simple goals that will improve the performance of those developers with less experience. Further improvements would be possible in future iterations. Therefore, we want students to commit at all, to commit more often, to commit more regularly, to write commit messages for their commits, and to write longer commit messages overall.

When defining the goal, PAIP requires the change agent to choose either one or both of "Start Adopting a New Practice" or "Improve Adoption of a Known Practice"; for our experiment, we choose both. In every previous instance of the software project course, there have been some students who never committed to version control, while most did commit at least once. Some of those committed only in bursts, some committed more regularly; some wrote commit messages, and some others did not. For the goals above, we therefore want to both *increase* adoption and *increase* adoption.

Research Questions

For the context of this evaluation, we formulate our goals into research questions that we will investigate in the succeeding section, documenting PAIP's sixth step:

- *RQ 1:* Does our intervention influence student developers to make more commits and space them out more evenly over time?

- *RQ 2:* Does our intervention influence student developers to write more and longer commit messages?

Defining the Metrics To measure our previously defined goals, we choose the metrics listed in Table 8.1. The table also assigns metrics to research questions. Most metrics are self-explanatory, except possibly the time between consecutive commits. We use this metric to measure whether developers commit more *regularly* — that is, more evenly spread out over time, with less *bursts* of commits. Assuming a constant number of commits, a more regular committing behavior would then result in the median time between commits to *increase*.

The final version of PAIP recommends choosing meaningful metrics that also cannot be manipulated, whereas the early version used in this experiment did not. Thus, the above metrics can be easily manipulated by simply committing more often without any reasonable content. Also, they do not state anything about the actual quality of a commit, and therefore do not carry much meaning. Section 8.3.3 provides insights into these issues with a qualitative analysis. However, we follow the *playful metric* recommendation in that we never connected the committing behavior of students with actual consequences, such as passing or failing the course.

Finally, PAIP also requires us to define when to take measurements and to record a baseline measurement. For this quasi-experiment, our baseline — i.e., the control group — consists of the Subversion repositories collected during previous instances of the course from 2007 to 2010. These repositories contain the commits of 214 students. The results are measured after the course has ended.

Hypotheses

For our experiment, we derive the alternative hypotheses for our research questions. We assume that a positive influence on the commit behavior of developers can be exerted by deploying our persuasive intervention. This influence should lead to more commits per developer, to temporally more evenly spaced commits, to more commits with messages per developer, and to longer commit messages. Accordingly, our respective null hypotheses are that the deployment of the intervention has no influence on these phenomena.

8.2.3. Choose Adoption Patterns

The previous two steps of applying PAIP reveal that we want to either start or improve the adoption of a practice that is comprised of relatively creative tasks. We assume to have some existing adopters. The meaning of our metrics is questionable, however the early version of PAIP did not yet recognize this. Based on this information, we choose the following adoption

RQ	Metric	Counting Rule
RQ 1	c	Number of commits per user
	$\Delta t_{C,avg}$	Average and median time between two consec-
	$\Delta t_{C,med}$	utive commits of a user in seconds
RQ 2	c_M	Number of commits with message per user
	c_M/c	Message-to-commit-ratio per user
	$l_{M,avg}$	Average and median number of characters of
	$l_{M,med}$	the commit messages of a user

Table 8.1.: *Summary of the defined metrics, assigned to their respective research questions.*

patterns for our intervention in the third step of PAIP. For each pattern, we also repeat its *solution* below.

- **Normative Behavior:** "Make explicit what normative behavior should be by continuously publishing the behavior of developers, positively emphasizing desirable behavior."

- **Triggers:** "Use notifications to cue developers to applying a practice by directing their attention to a task related to the practice. To support motivation, associate triggers with positive feedback or a goal to be reached. Do not overload developers with triggers."

- **Points & Levels:** "Award points and levels for the activity that is to be started or intensified. Provide a space for users to display their points and levels, e.g. on a user profile. Give clear instructions on how to attain different levels."

  Note that the recommendation for *clear instructions* was added only after the completion of this experiment, and therefore was not taken into account.

- **Leaderboard:** "Use a metric that measures compliance with the software engineering practice to rank developers against each other, creating explicit competition. If possible, have groups compete against each other instead of individual developers against each other."

  Note that the recommendation for *groups competing against each other* was added only after the completion of this experiment, and therefore was not taken into account.

- **Challenge:** "Provide developers with explicit, attainable, and challenging goals. Make sure developers understand what the conditions for attaining the goal are and give explicit feedback on results. Prefer challenges that require the developer to learn something new over those that merely require reaching a certain performance as measured by a metric."

  Note that the recommendation for *learning goals* was added only after the completion of this experiment, and therefore was not taken into account.

- **Progress Feedback:** "Provide developers with positive feedback on the progress they are making in their application of the practice."

- In addition, the early version of the list of adoption patterns contained a pattern that recommended *Commenting*: adding a commenting facility to the messages generated by the *Normative Behavior* adoption pattern to stimulate exchanges. This was indicated by results reported on by Foster et al. [64], however further evidence was not found in the literature review. This pattern was therefore not included in the adoption pattern catalog.

Except for the knowledge stage — which was not addressed by the early version of PAIP —, this selection of adoption patterns covers all stages of the innovation-decision process that are relevant to PAIP. Three of the patterns are from the *motivation* category: as mentioned before, we suspect missing motivation to be a reason for the adoption issues.

8.2.4. Design Treatment

Using the adoption patterns chosen in the previous step, we now create a treatment that implements the patterns. This design is in part informed by the examples listed for each adoption pattern.

Newsfeed   A newsfeed displaying the version control commits for each team implements the *Normative Behavior* adoption pattern. When no commit message is given, the application displays a highlighted text stating that a message is missing.

Leaderboard   A list of a team's members, ordered by their respective number of commits so far, implements the *Leaderboard* adoption pattern. Next to the name of each team member, the member's current number of commits is given. Below, the total number of commits for the team is displayed.

Milestones   At predefined thresholds for numbers of commits, the application congratulates users and teams on reaching a milestone. This implements the *Points & Levels* pattern. By slowly increasing the distance between the thresholds, this also implements the *Challenge* pattern: by committing, developers are able to recognize that there will be another milestone at an even higher number of commits, providing them with a goal. The congratulatory messages implement the *Progress Feedback* pattern.

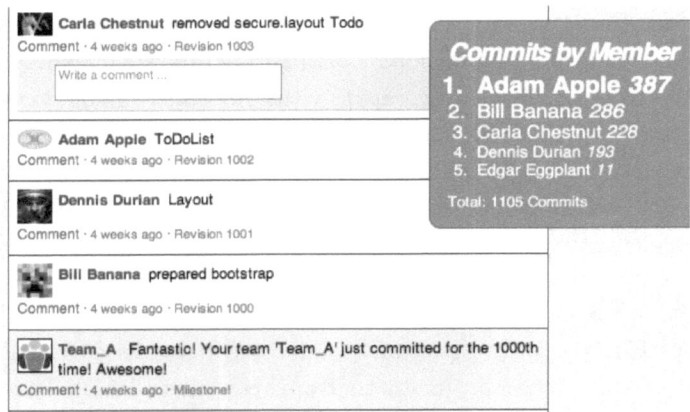

Figure 8.3: *A screenshot of Teamfeed's newsfeed and leaderboard.*

Notifications For positive events, such as reaching an individual or team milestone, the application sends out email notifications — this implements the *Triggers* adoption pattern. The congratulatory messages in the emails implement the *Progress Feedback* pattern.

Weekly Digest Each sunday, the application emails a weekly digest to each developer. It shows the current leaderboard, as well as any milestones reached in that week. This implements the *Triggers* adoption pattern. The congratulatory messages that were given when a milestone was reached implement the *Progress Feedback* pattern.

Teamfeed

We now present the completed Teamfeed application. As recommended by PAIP, it is a Web application. For notifications, it uses email. Teamfeed periodically reads the commits to each team's repository and saves them to a database. They are then displayed in a newsfeed for each team. Every student in the project can log in to Teamfeed using their Subversion account and is then presented with their respective team's newsfeed. The newsfeeds of other teams are not accessible to the students. Fig. 8.3 shows an anonymized screenshot of the application in which the names of students and their team have been altered. Several other texts have been translated from German into English.

```
Hello Edgar Eggplant!

In this weekly digest, we report what you and your team
achieved in the previous seven days.

You made 18 commits this weeks.

Your teammates achieved the following:
* Adam Apple made 36 commits this week and, in doing so,
reached a milestone: the 100th commit.
* Dennis Durian made 10 commits this week.
* Carla Chestnut made 32 commits this week.
* Bill Banana made 21 commits this week.

In total, your team made 117 commits this week. This allowed
you to reach a milestone: your 500th commit. Excellent!

This is the current status of your team:
    1. Dennis Durian (132)
    2. Adam Apple (122)
    3. Bill Banana (107)
    4. Carla Chestnut (84)
    5. Edgar Eggplant (66)

Best wishes for next week!
 The Teamfeed Team
 http://teamfeed.example.org
```

Figure 8.4: *A weekly digest as sent by Teamfeed.*

Reaching a milestone generates a special posts to the newsfeed. For the milestones, we defined thresholds of 1, 10, 25, 50, 100, 250, 500, 750, 1000, 1500, 2000, 2500, 3000, 4000, 5000, 7500, and 10000 commits. These generate posts such as *"Congratulations! Jane Doe has reached her 200th commit!"* or *"Wonderful! Your team has just reached the 1000th commit!"* We based the thresholds on previous semesters' commit counts and added a buffer.

On the right, the leaderboard lists the team members and the counts of their respective commits so far. For higher ranks, name and commit count are displayed in a larger font.

Each Sunday at around 3pm, Teamfeed sent out the weekly email digest to each student such as the one depicted in Fig. 8.4. The digest summarizes how many commits the individual student has made in the past week, but also provides this information about their teammates. It also mentions milestones that were reached during the week and shows the current state of the leaderboard.

8.2.5. Deploy Intervention

Once the treatments have been created, the change agent deploys them as a persuasive intervention in the organization. We deployed *Teamfeed* at the

Group		Control					Teamfeed
Term	2007	2008	2009	2010	Σ		2011
n	40	40	76	58	214		37
n_C	31	36	73	55	195		37
$n - n_C$	9	4	3	3	19		0
n_C/n	78%	90%	96%	95%	91%		100%
c_{total}	3973	3680	6993	7223	21869		4842
c_{total}/n	99	92	92	125	102		131

Table 8.2.: *Overview of data sources and their values for number of subjects (n), number of subjects who committed (n_C), number of subjects who never committed ($n - n_C$), percentage of committing subjects (n_C/n), number of total commits (c_{total}), and average commits per subject (c_{total}/n).*

start of the software project course in the fall term of 2011. The students were told that the purpose of Teamfeed was to support their collaboration.

8.3. Analysis

The final stage of PAIP involves taking a measurement and comparing it to the baseline to assess the effectiveness of the intervention. This informs the next iteration of the process.

Table 8.2 shows the data sources we used for data collection in our experiment. It includes the data from five years of the software project course, i.e., the data accumulated in the fall terms of the years 2007 through 2011. The first four years were used as the control group. In 2011, we introduced the Teamfeed application and therefore used it as our treatment group.

In total, there were 26711 commits in the five years (c_{total}). In the first four years, each participant made 102 commits on average (c_{total}/n). In 2011, this value was at 131 commits. 251 students took the course over the five years, which can be seen as n in Table 8.2. The treatment group consisted of 37 participants.

n_C documents the number of students that did commit at all in the respective year. As the values for n_C/n show, all students in the treatment group committed at least once to version control (100%). In the previous years, however, some participants never made a single commit (i.e., on average, 91% committed at least once).

Fig. 8.5 illustrates the commit behavior by the control group (*Regular*) and the treatment group (*Teamfeed*) over time. Special events, such as

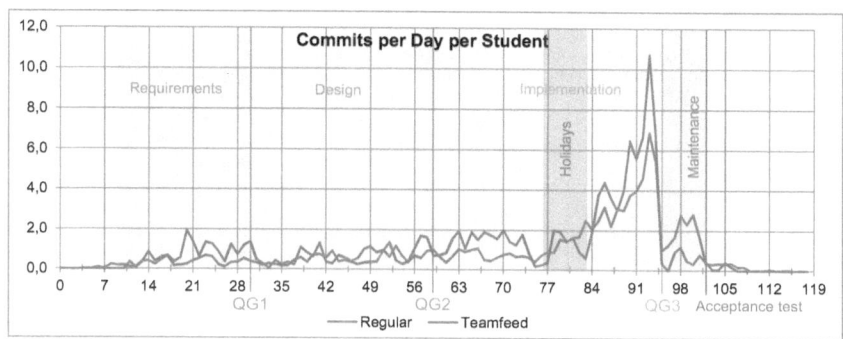

Figure 8.5: *Commits of the control group (Control) and the treatment group (Teamfeed) over time.*

quality gates — i.e., ends of phases — and Christmas holidays can be seen as variations in the graph.

For example, for all five years, the number of commits spiked in the implementation phase, and even more so shortly before the end of the phase. During the holidays, no considerable decline can be seen. Then, after New Year, commit activity rises sharply. It is visible in the graph that the treatment group exhibited a more active commit behavior before the holidays, but a relative decline in the maintenance phase.

8.3.1. Descriptive Statistics

We now present the data we collected for the metrics we defined, aggregated in Table 8.3 and visualized as box plots in Fig. 8.6. Each set of data is declared for the control group (C) and the treatment group (T), respectively. For each value, we provide the minimum, the median, and the maximum value.

For example, Table 8.3 shows a 76% increase in median commits per participant (c) for the treatment group. The ratio of commits with messages to commits overall (c_M/c) increased by 75%. We now discuss whether these and other differences are statistically significant.

8.3.2. Hypothesis Testing

For most metrics, we were able to determine a statistically significant difference between the values for the control group and the values for the

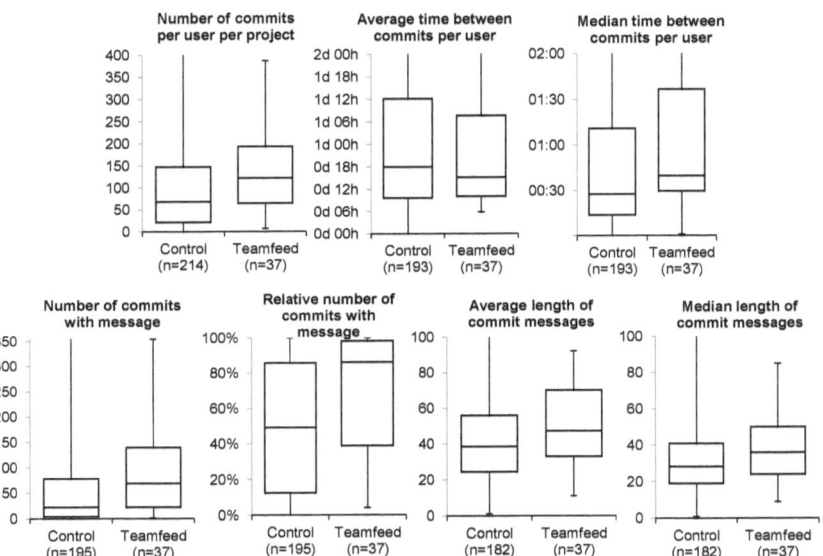

Figure 8.6: *Box plots of the data collected for the metrics.*

Metric	Group	Min	Median	Max
c	Control (n=214)	0	69	683
	Treatment (n=37)	7	122	387
$\Delta t_{C,avg}$	C (n=193)	00:00	17:55	>17d
hh:mm	T (n=37)	05:51	15:09	>8d
$\Delta t_{C,med}$	C (n=193)	00:00	00:27	>6d
hh:mm	T (n=37)	00:00	00:39	>1d
c_M	C (n=195)	0	22	587
	T (n=37)	1	69	354
c_M/c	C (n=195)	0%	49%	100%
	T (n=37)	4%	86%	100%
$l_{M,avg}$	C (n=182)	1	39	211
	T (n=37)	11	47	92
$l_{M,med}$	C (n=182)	1	28	165
	T (n=37)	9	36	85

Table 8.3.: *Minimum, median, and maximum values for the collected metrics: number of commits per subject (c), average ($\Delta t_{C,avg}$) as well as median ($\Delta t_{C,med}$) time between commits, number of commits with a message per subject (c_M), percentage of commits with a message (c_M/c), and average ($l_{M,avg}$) as well as median ($l_{M,med}$) lengths of commit messages.*

treatment group. We performed a Kolmogorov-Smirnov normality test for all the metrics. These tests showed that the data do not follow a normal distribution. Therefore, we had to use the non-parametric two-tailed Mann-Whitney U test to test for the significances of differences. Table 8.4 presents the results of our tests for statistical significance.

For research question 1, there is a significant difference between the number of commits per student for the two groups: an increase in 76% ($c; p < 0.01$). The average time between commits does not differ significantly ($\Delta t_{C,avg}$). However, the median time between commits exhibits a significant ($\Delta t_{C,med}; p < 0.05$) difference: an increase in 44%. We therefore reject the null hypotheses for the first and the third metrics of research question 1.

The measurements for research question 2 show significant differences. The number of commits with messages per developer increased by 213% ($c_M; p < 0.01$); the ratio of commits with messages to overall commits increased by 75% ($c_M/c; p < 0.01$).

The difference for the average length of commit messages is not significant, with a 20% increase ($l_{M,avg}; p < 0.1$). The difference for the median length of commit messages is significant with a 28% increase ($l_{M,med}; p < 0.05$). We therefore reject three of the four null hypotheses for research question 2.

8.3.3. Qualitative Analysis

To better understand the effects of our intervention, we now provide an additional qualitative discussion.

RQ	Metric	Control	Treatment	Difference	Confidence
RQ 1	c	69	122	+76%	$p < 0.01$
	$\Delta t_{C,avg}$	17:55	15:09	-15%	$p > 0.1$
	$\Delta t_{C,med}$	00:27	00:39	+44%	$p < 0.05$
RQ 2	c_M	22	69	+213%	$p < 0.01$
	c_M/c	49%	86%	+75%	$p < 0.01$
	$l_{M,avg}$	39	47	+20%	$p < 0.1$
	$l_{M,med}$	28	36	+28%	$p < 0.05$

Table 8.4.: *Overview of statistical test results.*

LID Sessions At the end of the LID sessions we conducted with each team of the treatment group, we inquired about their impressions of Teamfeed [164]. This provided us with some notable insights:

- More experienced developers often ignored Teamfeed and the emails it sent. Some even had setup a filter in their email clients for this purpose. However, only few seemed to be annoyed by the emails. In an industrial setting, one might want to give developers a way to opt out of such email. Yet, none asked us about such an option during the course.

- Several of the more novice developers reported that they felt motivated by the milestones. The only team which reached the *1000 commits* milestone was comprised of such members.

- No developer reported any manipulative attempts by themselves or by team mates. To ensure this, we performed a sanity check of a sample of commits, finding no indication for manipulation (such as empty commits).

- One developer explicitly said that Teamfeed's milestones made him commit in smaller batches. Instead of putting several bug fixes into a single commit, he committed his changes after every single fix. In our view, this is desirable behavior for centralized version control systems.

Website Access To assess whether participants used Teamfeed at all, we measured its usage. Fig. 8.7 shows the daily page views over time. While usage is moderately strong during the requirements phase, it goes down in November. Both phases were focused on the creation of documents, and after a while the application's novelty might have worn off. When software development activities became more important, though, page views went up at the start of December and remained strong for the rest of the project. This indicates that the Teamfeed application was actually used by the project participants, which we additionally ensured by scrutinizing the web server's log data manually.

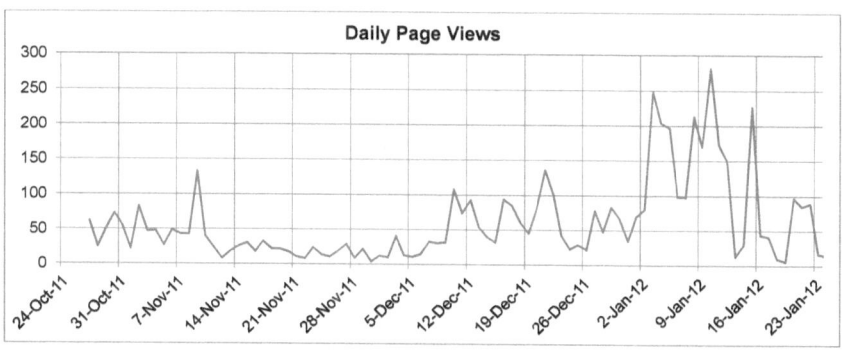

Figure 8.7: *Daily page views for the Teamfeed application.*

8.3.4. Research Questions

In our research question 1 we asked: *Does our intervention influence student developers to make more commits and space them out more evenly over time?*

To answer this question, we defined three metrics: the number of commits per student, the average time between commits, and the median time between commits. Based on our measurements, we were able to reject the null hypothesis for the first and the third metrics. Therefore, we conclude that our treatment was indeed able to influence student developers to make more commits and space them out more evenly over time. Not only did it lead to a significantly higher number of commits per developer, but also resulted in a more evenly distributed time between commits.

Research question 2 asked: *Does our intervention influence student developers to write more and longer commit messages?*

For this question, we defined four metrics: the number of commits with messages, the ratio of commits with messages to overall commits, the average length of commit messages, and the median length of commit messages. For three of these metrics, we were able to reject the null hypothesis. We conclude that the introduction of our application did indeed influence student developers to write more and longer commit messages. More commits contained commit messages at all, and those that did contained longer messages.

8.4. Threats to Validity

This section discusses threats to the validity of our quasi-experiment. We show how we tried to minimize them through the experiment design and mention remaining limitations.

8.4.1. Internal Validity

A significant difference between the control group and the treatment group does not in itself represent a causal relationship between our intervention and the differences in measurement. Other confounding factors might have had an influence. The population itself, the students' education, and our behavior towards the students might all have been different.

The advantage of using different populations for the control and treatment groups, however, is that there should have been no confounding effects with regard to learning or maturation. In addition, we took care to execute the course the same as in previous years. As our group also provides the basic software engineering courses, we feel qualified to say that we did not notice any notable differences in the students from the control group compared to the students in the treatment group. Additionally, our courses provide the basic education on version control, which was the same for both groups.

Three of the seven development teams of the treatment group used the Dropbox[4] service to share files with each other. For the previous years, we did not notice any use of Dropbox or alternative file sharing services by the teams: to the best of our knowledge, they shared files using their Subversion repositories. The use of Dropbox by members of the treatment group might have *decreased* the use of version control.

8.4.2. Construct Validity

Whether the practices we chose for version control are preferable in a given software engineering situation is debatable. However, we consider them an important step for the population we investigated. Populations at other levels of version control proficiency may require different interventions. Even though the use of metrics in software development can be problematic [18], our research questions and the metrics we derived address the adoption of

---

[4]http://dropbox.com

these practices as directly as possible. We therefore consider them appropriate.

In a future investigation, we plan to examine any quality differences in the commits and commit messages of the control and treatment groups. A preliminary investigation of commit messages showed indications for a decrease of nonsense messages ("hahaha!"), a decrease of purely technical messages ("add getter getUser()") and an increase in mentions of functional changes ("fix incompatibility with framework version 1.2.5").

One possible effect of public, competitive metrics is that people try to "game the system" — i.e., they try to increase their value for the metric using the easiest strategies, which might often not be what the creators of the system intended. In our case, these would be empty commits or nonsense commits. To rule this effect out, we randomly sampled some of the commits from our treatment group. We found no indications for invalid or manipulative commits.

8.4.3. Conclusion Validity

To mitigate threats to conclusion validity, we used the data collected over several years of the software project course for our control group. These 214 participants, combined with 37 participants in the treatment group, were suitable to provide statistically significant results. To decrease the risk of manual errors, all data were collected automatically.

8.4.4. External Validity

The participants of our experiment were mostly students of computer science in their 5th semester. As the German Bachelor of Science degree lasts 6 semesters, most students were almost finished with their studies. As our treatment was directed at issues with version control practices we had experienced from similar populations, we cannot generalize this concrete intervention to different populations. Another application of PAIP, while more elaborate than a simple transfer of the intervention, would be more sensible.

It is questionable how many metrics and additional interventions can be introduced before software developers start ignoring such measures. The tolerable amount of such treatments might be very low. Further research regarding such scenarios is warranted.

Similarly, our software projects are restricted to a single semester, i.e., about four months. We do not think that our experiment can be generalized to much longer runtimes, as potential numbing effects seem plausible. Again, further research is needed in this regard.

8.5. Conclusions

Our quasi-experiment demonstrated that PAIP and the catalog of adoption patterns can be used to improve the adoption of software engineering practices — in this case, the commit behavior of student developers. While we tried to design our experiment to minimize threats to validity, some of them were beyond our control. It is therefore still possible that the effects we measured were created or influenced by other, confounding factors. However, the qualitative data from the LID sessions back our interpretation. Indeed, some students reported in the LID sessions that they were more likely to commit more often and to take greater care when writing their commit messages because of the added publicity, an effect that Dabbish et al. [38] report for GitHub.

We systematically combined adoption patterns that were appropriate for our context and goals, creating a persuasive intervention. Even though PAIP still requires the change agent to work creatively when translating the adoption patterns into features of a treatment, the process is now based on less speculation than it would be without PAIP and the adoption patterns.

By using the catalog of adoption patterns, we accessed a reusable repository of effects that can improve the adoption of a practice. The patterns we used supported motivation by providing developers with goals, facilitated social learning and related mechanisms, and regularly triggered developers to revisit Teamfeed.

This specific intervention worked for less experienced software developers in a university setting. As we argued in section 8.4, the intervention itself might not generalize. However, this is exactly what PAIP intends: it provides a way to create interventions that are tailored to a practice, an adoption problem, a population, and adoption goals.

Our quasi-experiment has shown that the application of PAIP is feasible and can be effective. While this need not be true for every possible adoption problem or situation, this data point serves as a good indicator. More evaluations in different contexts would be needed to improve confidence in this regard. However, this was not feasible within the constraints of this thesis.

9. Related Work

This chapter presents related work from software engineering, CSCW, and human-computer interaction. These works either use means similar to those used in this thesis to reach their goals, or pursue related goals.

9.1. Adoption Research in Software Engineering

Meyerovich and Rabkin [120] discuss programming language adoption and use the diffusion of innovations theory as their model. They propose a comprehensive research agenda that addresses how programming language adoption should be studied. Among other means, the authors propose improving language adoption by leveraging social networks for persuasion.

The scope of this research, however, is for now restricted to programming languages as opposed to practices. Another differentiator with regard to this thesis is their intention to also influence language design to optimize for adoption. Conversely, the approach presented in this thesis is focused on *not* changing existing practices, but on augmenting their environment. The fact that Meyerovich and Rabkin are proposing a research agenda for future investigations demonstrates the relevance and timeliness of the research reported on in this thesis.

9.2. Community Design

Several authors use means that are similar to those proposed in this thesis — mechanisms from collaboration design and social media — to inform the design of communities and collaborative support systems. This section introduces a selection of such approaches.

Kraut et al. [95] provide a list of what they call *design claims* that are based on research results to guide the design of online communities. The authors organize their claims into the following categories:

1. ***Starting new online communities:*** When a new online community is created, reaching critical mass with regard to members and content can be crucial to make it attractive to potential users.

2. ***Dealing with newcomers:*** New members have not yet learned the conventions that are in place in a community and do not yet have strong ties to its members. This category discusses how such problems can be addressed.

3. ***Encouraging commitment:*** Compared to employment at a company or being a member of a local support group, membership in an online community is relatively fragile. Members can leave at will, for example for comparable alternative communities.

4. ***Encouraging contribution:*** Undercontribution can be a problem in online communities: a community's value to its members rests on contributions such as conversations, collaborations, or uploaded media. Yet only very few members contribute anything substantial.

5. ***Regulating behavior:*** Manipulative or abusive behaviors such as spamming can be a problem for the health of an online community. The design claims in this category show how such issues can be mitigated.

These design claims are related to this thesis' adoption patterns in that they employ similar mechanisms — some of the research the design claims are based on was even used in the creation of the adoption patterns. However, while Kraut et al. [95] provide very actionable advise for researchers and practitioners interested in creating and managing online communities, the problems their design claims address are only partially related to the issues addressed by this thesis.

In a relatively high-level discussion, Benkler [14] contrasts the different belief systems that perceive work as either mandatory and unenjoyable or as deliberate and fulfilling. Arguing for the latter, he shows how collaboration facilitated by computers and the Internet creates and enables new models of work. He closes with a discussion of the means that are available to system designers to support deliberate cooperation.

Philosophically, Benkler's contribution is related to this thesis' proposal: mandating the adoption of a practice only works to a certain degree, collaborative creative work must be a deliberate effort to reach its full potential. However, Benkler's recommendations are much more general than the adoption patterns derived in chapter 7: they are meant to applied when "designing for cooperation". Furthermore, the recommendations are very broad and abstract, in that they provide no directly actionable advice for designers of cooperation systems.

Cuel et al. [36] use insights about human motivation to provide guidelines for designing community systems in which volunteers create semantic annotations of content. While the goal of this approach clearly differs from this thesis' goal, the mechanisms used are related. The authors propose using Participatory Design [157] when creating volunteer communities, arguing that user involvement will increase motivation. In addition, they propose a set of guidelines to support both intrinsic and extrinsic motivations in the final systems.

PAIP similarly encourages user involvement, but in a more light-weight manner. The guidelines proposed by Cuel et al. are more abstract than the adoption patterns provided by this thesis, and thus should be less actionable. Overall, the presented approach is based on a set of theories on motivation. In addition, Cuel et al. frame the addressed problem as one of Game Theory [66], which assumes rational agents. However, as Benkler [14] argues in his discussion of community design, humans cannot be assumed to be acting rationally, and approaches designing for cooperation or motivation need to take this into account.

9.3. Persuasive Technology

Persuasive Technology uses computer software to influence the decisions, attitudes, and behaviors of individuals. Fogg [62] provides a broad overview of the field, which he calls *captology*. In this context, Fogg defines persuasion as "an attempt to change attitudes or behaviors or both (without using coercion or deception)." Similar to PAIP, captology uses non-coercive means, however with much broader goal. As opposed to this thesis' approach, captology focuses on the interaction between an individual and a computer program, not on the interaction between individuals *through* computer programs. A few approaches mentioned by Fogg, however, leverage the effects of social learning, social influence, and social comparison.

9.4. Gamification

This thesis' approach is related to *gamification*, which, according to Deterding et al. [50], is "the use of game design elements in non-game contexts." Gamification is used to motivate individuals to engage in activities that are *not* games. While several proponents of gamification reduce it to simply adding badges, ranks, leaderboards, points, etc. to existing activities, some are more serious and base their approach on accepted theories of games, play, social psychology, and the psychology of motivation.

The fields of application for gamification are diverse: some use it to motivate users to use mobile applications more, others use it to cultivate healthier lifestyles. Gamification does not need to be implemented in software systems; instead, complete business processes might be redesigned based on its principles. Alternatively, a gamification intervention may consist mostly of hardware, such as stairs redesigned as huge and functional pianos that motivate pedestrians to take the stairs instead of the escalator [191]. Deterding and colleagues recently discussed the current state of gamification as a field [49].

The approach presented in this thesis has a certain overlap with gamification, in that some mechanisms that are used by some of the adoption patterns are also used in gamification. However, while this thesis' approach might propose elements that might appear game-like at times — such as rankings or badges — it is not based on game- or play-related theories.

Simple examples of gamification in software engineering practices include TDGotchi[1] — "a virtual pet that helps you raise your TDD practice" — and the addition of game elements to software development activities by Passos et al. [137]. In their case study, they applied mechanisms related to the *Points & Levels*, *Automatic Badges*, and *Leaderboard* adoption patterns presented in this thesis.

9.5. Incentive Strategies in Knowledge Management

Davenport and Probst [41] document several cases of knowledge sharing systems at Siemens. To motivate employees to share their knowledge, most approaches provided extrinsic rewards in form of monetary bonuses or points that could be exchanged for real goods. As Deci and Ryan [44] have shown, a legitimate use case for providing extrinsic rewards is jumpstarting a new behavior, which was the case at Siemens. Yet, extrinsic rewards are not sustainable. However, the long-term effects of the rewards on knowledge management at Siemens are not reported. Sometimes, competition between teams developed; however that only seemed to occur incidentally and was

---

[1]http://www.happyprog.com/tdgotchi

not planned for. In summary, the approaches at Siemens used rather simple motivators, did not handle motivation in a systematic manner, and their sustainability remains doubtful.

Dencheva et al. [48] have used reputation — i.e., identity transparency — and a theory of human motivation to increase the quantity and quality of contributions to a corporate knowledge sharing Wiki. While knowledge management is a relevant subject for software engineering, these efforts as well have not been as systematic and broad as this thesis' approach.

9.6. Theory W

Theory W by Boehm and Ross [17] is a management theory focused on software development projects. It is a successor to several other theories:

- According to **Theory X**, management should coerce workers into performing their assigned tasks. The ideal workers are running "smoothly as machines". This stifles creativity and adaptability.

- To address this shortcoming, **Theory Y** focuses on stimulating creativity and individual initiative. However, this leads to conflicts and coordination problems.

- **Theory Z** attempts to counter these challenges by emphasizing the creation of a corporate culture with shared values to avoid conflicts. However, Theory Z ignores interactions between organizations and individual projects.

Theory W argues that to successfully executing development projects, the manager should strive to "make everyone a winner" [17]. In this context, our approach enables managers to make the software developers winners — by providing them with practices and tools that target their motivations. More concretely, the approach proposed by this thesis would support the first step from Theory W: "Establish a set of win-win preconditions".

9.7. Summary

This section has presented research related to the contributions of this thesis. Some approaches use similar mechanisms, and some address similar problems. However, no prior publications were found that use persuasive interventions such as those proposed in this thesis to improve the adoption of software engineering practices.

The following chapter concludes this thesis and provides an outlook to future work.

10. Conclusions & Outlook

This chapter first discusses the limitations of the approach presented in this thesis and the research methods used to create it. The second section provides pointers for promising research avenues that this thesis enables or that could augment the presented results. Finally, a summary of the contributions of this thesis is provided.

10.1. Limitations

As any applied research, the results of this thesis have some limitations that may constrain their applicability or reliability.

One of the basic assumptions of this thesis is that the software engineering practices for which adoption should be improved cannot be changed — they have to be accepted as they are given. This may constrain the effectiveness of the approach. By relaxing this requirement, different results might be achievable. However, the adoption patterns are meant to be applicable to *any* software engineering practice. Permitting changes in the practices would require the adoption patterns to be more abstract, as they would have to include recommendations on *how* to modify any existing practice. Another alternative would be constraining the approach to only a certain class of practices. This is a trade-off, and this thesis takes a position on this continuum that enables it to be applicable to a broad set of software engineering practices, while still providing relatively concrete adoption patterns.

The list of adoption patterns may not be complete. To achieve breadth, the literature review from which the patterns were derived had to compromise on verifiable completeness. It is possible that the literature review missed patterns that would have been supportive of the thesis' goals. Future research might evolve the current list of patterns — adding, modifying, or removing patterns based on new insights. However, as chapter 8 has shown, the current list of adoption patterns can already be effective.

All adoption patterns are based on existing research that achieved desirable results — however, not necessarily with software engineering subjects, or with the goal of improving the adoption of practices by individuals. Therefore, the patterns might not work in every situation. Company culture, politics, and of course human beings all have high degrees of variance. Again, this is a conscious trade-off: to achieve a very high reliability and predictability of an adoption pattern's effects, it would need to be restricted to only very specific contexts for which it has already been shown to be effective. This would severely constrain the applicability of this thesis' contributions.

This thesis provides only the evaluation of an early version of the process and a selection of patterns documented in chapter 8. It would be beneficial to conduct more evaluations to assess the final version of PAIP and possibly evolving it further. In addition, multiple additional evaluations of each adoption pattern in different situations and for different goals would increase the dependability of this thesis' contribution. This is a subject for future research.

10.2. Outlook

Technology influences society, and society in turn also influences technology, creating a feedback loop that constantly changes the environment in which technology exists [115]. This requires constant adaption and reevaluation of research that leverages or supports social processes. Therefore, the list of adoption patterns should evolve with future developments in software engineering, social media, HCI, CSCW, psychology, sociology, and possibly other research fields. However, while the concrete adoption patterns in this thesis may evolve, the general approach of supporting adoption with the systematic design of cooperative systems should be relatively stable even in the future.

The approach presented in this thesis is focused on supporting the adoption of *software engineering* practices by developers. However, several insights from this research should also be of value to other disciplines. The core idea of this thesis is that the systematic design of cooperative systems based on empirical evidence can improve cooperation and influence individuals in a constructive manner. This strategy can also be used in other domains and other goals.

Some of the adoption patterns presented in this thesis could be used to improve employee motivation and morale — especially the patterns from the motivation category could be suitable for this goal. However, in every category of the adoption pattern catalog, there are adoption patterns that can support at least one of competence, relatedness, or autonomy. As such, many more adoption patterns than only those from the motivation category could be used. Therefore, this approach could be part of a different approach to employee management, which Benkler [14] as well as Amabile and Kramer [6] sketched in their recent publications. When employees are provided with autonomy and a supportive social environment, cooperation, creativity, learning, and innovation are more likely to result. Software engineering has strong requirements regarding these aspects.

The empirical studies presented in this thesis (cf. chapter 5) have revealed several challenges and opportunities related to the design of cooperative software, and to the diffusion of software engineering practices and technologies. For example, can the drive-by commits found in section 5.2 be leveraged to improve testing practices in companies? How can we support software developers using social media to assess software engineering innovations such as libraries and frameworks? Which signals do they use to assess reliability or dependability before deciding for a library, and what are the consequences of such assessments? Future research will need to consider such questions in more depth.

Finally, the approach presented in this thesis uses insights about the design of cooperative systems to improve software engineering. This may be applicable vice versa: software engineering, which emphasizes the *systematic* creation of software, should be applied to the design of cooperative systems. The collection of design claims by Kraut et al. [95] provides a starting point for this, and this thesis contributes another one. The design of cooperative systems is still a bit of an art — social processes are complicated and, especially in engineering, not well understood. However, approaches like the one presented in this thesis can support making it *less* of an art, and more of a systematic approach.

10.3. Contributions

This thesis contributes an approach that supports the adoption of software engineering practices by software developers in a systematic manner. It does so in a non-coercive manner, providing some advantages over existing coercive approaches — namely, facilitating creativity, autonomy, and other crucial components of successful software development.

Two empirical studies uncover opportunities showing that the design of cooperative systems can improve the adoption of practices and technologies in software engineering. These insights culminate in a broad literature review, from which a catalog of adoption patterns is derived. PAIP, a process based on existing software process improvement models, enables a systematic application of these patterns in organizations. An evaluation of the approach in a quasi-experiment shows significant improvements for the adoption of version control practices among student developers.

The approach presented in this thesis is independent of concrete software engineering practices. As such, organizations will be able to apply it to their adoption challenges even when the state of the art in software engineering practices has changed.

However, the contributions of this thesis to software engineering research transcend the presented core approach. By exploring the influence of social media on software developers and software engineering, several opportunities for future research have been uncovered.

A. Testing on GitHub — Coding System

This appendix contains the coding system that was developed in the study reported on in section 5.2. Each category contains concepts, which themselves contain codes. Some codes appeared in other concepts from time to time; this appendix nests codes into the concepts they appeared in most commonly.

A.1. Category: Interaction

How do developers on GitHub interact with each other, and what do they consider to be special about GitHub in this regard?

A.1.1. Concept: Characteristics of Code Changes

When interacting with others on GitHub, developers use certain properties of code, e.g. of proposed changes, to guide their behavior.

Code	Description
change size	Smaller changes might not be scrutinized as extensively by project owners.
change target	The target of a change — e.g. an important class or a CSS file — may determine the level of scrutiny a project owner invests for a pull request.
change type	Project owners used the type of a change — e.g. whether it touched important business logic or only slightly changed the application's appearance — to determine how thoroughly the change would need to be tested.
testing effort	If a pull request's testing effort would be relatively high compared to the change, some project owners waived their testing demands.

A.1.2. Concept: Characteristics of People

When interacting with others on GitHub, developers use certain properties of people to guide their behavior.

Code	Description
trust	Some project owners simply accepted pull requests if they came from a developer they trusted.

A.2. Category: Motivation

What are the motivations of project owners and contributors on GitHub for their behaviors with regard to testing?

A.2.1. Concept: Easier Maintenance

Some project owners said that tests would make maintenance easier.

Code	Description
support effort	Testing decreases the support effort.
tests as docs	Tests may serve as code documentation.
communicating requirements	Tests may communicate requirements; contributing a test may simply mean adding one's requirements to a project.

A.2.2. Concept: Project Domain

Some developers said that a project's domain — e.g. whether it was a testing framework or a web application for hobbyists — would influence their perception of whether the project should have a test suite.

Code	Description
role model	When their project was related to testing, project owners felt they should act as a role model for others.
domain oblige	Project owners felt obliged to write tests when their project was related to testing.
contributing oblige	Contributors felt obliged to write tests when a project was related to testing.

A.2.3. Concept: Implicit Communication

Developers claimed that they received and also sent several implicit cues when communicating testing culture.

Code	Description
existence of tests	Existing tests communicate that the project values testing.
prominent placement of tests	The prominent placement of tests in a project supports communicating that testing is valued.
show value	Some contributors tried communicating their own contribution's value by writing tests that highlighted it.

A.3. Category: Problems

What problems do members of GitHub encounter that are related to testing?

A.3.1. Concept: High Exposure

Project owners were sometimes struggling with the high exposure that GitHub provided their projects with.

Code	Description
scale	Project owners reported that at some point, their project had reached a scale that forced them to automate testing.
contributor churn	The ease of contributing on GitHub increases contributor churn, making it more important to communicate testing culture efficiently.
need automation	Some project owners without automated tests felt an urgent need for such a test suite.

A.3.2. Concept: Lacking Communication of Culture

Project owners as well as contributors mentioned that testing culture does not always get communicated properly.

Code	Description
no existing tests	Not having tests in a project communicates that the project does not necessarily value testing.
culture struggle	Some projects were struggling with creating an appropriate testing culture.
voluntarism	The high level of voluntarism in open source software development made project owner's reluctant to simply *demand* tests from contributors.
high barriers	Some developers reported that the barriers especially for first-time contributors were sometimes too high, e.g. because of a complicated testing setup.

A.4. Category: Coping

How do members of GitHub cope with challenges, and how does GitHub support its members?

A.4.1. Concept: Lowering Barriers

Developers tried to lower barriers for each other to make contribution and the acceptance of contributions easier.

Code	Description
CI service	Having a continuous integration service made accepting changes easier for project owners, likewise the integration of Travis CI with GitHub lowered the barrier for project owners to get started with CI.
humble PO	Instead of firmly demanding tests, project owners sometimes communicated more humbly with contributors, e.g. by kindly asking for tests.
PO writes tests	If a contributor did not include tests with their contributions, and the project owner was not able to convince the contributor to add tests, some project owners resorted to writing the missing tests themselves.
documented framework	Contributors reported that established and documented testing frameworks made it easier for them to include tests in their contributions.

A.4.2. Concept: Communication of Testing Culture

Some project owners actively tried to communicate their project's testing culture.

Code	Description
learning resources	To help potential contributor, some project owners took care to provide easy access to learning resources for testing, e.g. by linking to documentation of the testing framework used.
active support	Some project owners actively mentored new contributors to help them write tests for their contributions, e.g. via email, text chat, or Skype.
testing desired	Some project owners tried to make it obvious to new contributors that testing is desired in their projects.
lead by example	Some project owners said that they were trying to lead by example, i.e., they wrote tests and hoped that contributors would imitate them.
display testing signals	Some project owners and developers felt that simple testing signals, such as the CI status of a project, should be displayed prominently for a project. This would show that the project values testing.

A.5. Category: Impact

Which impact do interactions on GitHub, motivations, problems, and coping strategies have on open source development on GitHub?

A.5.1. Concept: Communication of Testing Culture

To support their project's contributors, project owners consciously changed their behavior to better communicate the project's testing culture. This allowed it to diffuse to developers, who would in turn adopt it and its values.

Code	Description
testing guidelines	Providing developers with testing guidelines makes the project's testing culture explicit and gives them a starting point to learn about it.
active communication	Project owners reported that they were trying to actively communicate their project's testing requirements.
pride	Some developers felt proud when they knew that they obliged with a project's testing culture.
direct exchanges	Direct exchanges between developers on GitHub were also said to be conductive to diffusing testing culture.
having a test suite	For developers, an existing test suite communicated that tests were indeed desired for new contributions.

A.5.2. Concept: New Risks

Some project owners and contributors saw some risks in the testing style that they perceived as prevalent on GitHub.

Code	Description
false sense of security	Some developers mentioned that test suites could lead to a false sense of security, as some might not check whether new contributions that did not include any new tests were even covered by existing tests.
happy path testing	Some developers criticized what they called a culture of "happy path testing" — testing only *desired* behavior, but not undesirable behavior or edge cases.
defer testing for traction	To help their project gain traction, some project owners consciously deferred testing and did not demand tests from contributors.

A.5.3. Concept: Exploration & Experimentation

For some, tests lowered the barriers to exploration and experimentation, and, therefore, to contributing to a project.

Code	Description
fast feedback through CI	A continuous integration server provides fast feedback when changing source code, this supports experimentation.
language ecosystem	Ruby was mentioned as having an ecosystem that supported exploration and experimentation through the easy development and testing setup many projects provide.
drive-by commit	The low barriers and the centralization of GitHub allowed developers to make contributions to a project without becoming involved with it.

A.5.4. Concept: Reputation

Testing was perceived as a noble activity that could increase a developer's or a project's reputation.

Code	Description
finding work	Some developers submitted pull-requests to respected (and well-tested) projects to improve their chances on the job market.
project reputation	Some project owners felt that they would have to write tests for their project so their projects' and their own reputations in the community would not suffer.
quality as ad	For companies, having tests in their open source projects can be an advertisement for their products, but also for potential employees that are looking for a company using good practices.

B. Mutual Assessment — Coding System

This appendix contains the coding system that was developed in the study reported on in section 5.3. Each category contains concepts, which themselves contain codes. Some codes appeared in other concepts from time to time; this appendix nests codes into the concepts they appeared in most commonly. For readability, some codes are repeated across concepts, e.g. when they applied to different actors.

B.1. Category: Interaction

How do participants of the social programer ecosystem interact with each other?

B.1.1. Concept: Assessment

Developers were assessing each other using different signals.

Code	Description
assess others	Developers were assessing other developers.
trusting quant	Some developers trusted the quantified activities displayed on Masterbranch and Coderwall.
footprint	Developers assessed others by what one developer called their "coder footprint" — an intuitive grasp of what kinds of technologies and projects someone was working on.
personal brand	Some developers explicitly said that they were managing their personal brands.

Similarly, recruiters were also assessing developers.

Code	Description
seeking passion	Some recruiters said they were looking for passionate developers.
identifying learners	Some recruiters said they were trying to identify fast learners.
seeking diversity	Some recruiters said they were looking for diversity in developers.

B.1.2. Concept: Connecting

Developers used social media to connect with other developers.

Code	Description
connecting interests	Developers said they participated in social media to connect with others through common interests.
personal network	Some developers used social media to utilize personal connections and word-of-mouth.
global ties	Some developers used social media for connecting with developers outside of their own local group.
enjoying recognition	Developers used social media because they enjoyed recognition from peers.
competition	Developers used social media — and especially Masterbranch or Coderwall — for competing with others and comparing themselves with them.
giving recognition	Some developers said they participated in social media to recognize good work of others.
motivating others	Some developers took part in social media for motivating peers to take part in open source.

B.1.3. Concept: Avoidance

Some developers consciously avoided certain areas of the social media space.

Code	Description
avoiding recruiters	Some developers actively tried to avoid recruiters.
avoiding aggressive communities	Some developers consciously avoided aggressive communities.

B.1.4. Concept: Filters

Recruiters described an approach to assessment that consisted of two layers: they would first filter out potential candidates based on relatively superficial signals.

Code	Description
skill lists	Recruiters used skill lists as a first filter when assessing potential candidates.
certifications	Recruiters used certifications as a first filter when assessing potential candidates.
OSS activity check	Open source activity and engagement sometimes acted as a baseline check.
social media check	Developers' activities on GitHub, Twitter, and StackOverflow were sometimes as more concrete baseline checks.
generic SNS	Some recruiters said they were using generic professional networking services, such as LinkedIn.
assess youth	Some recruiters openly said that they were assessing developers based on youth, as young people would be more open to new employers, relocating, and other requirements of the technology industry.

B.1.5. Concept: Lacking Trust in Signals

After using filters (above), recruiters would dig deeper, as they did not trust these simplified signals completely (see also: *Concept: Assessment* above).

Code	Description
digging deeper	Recruiters dug deeper after applying the aforementioned filters.
good practices	Recruiters used social media to observe developers using good practices and took that as a sign for good developers.
social skills	Recruiters tried using social media to assess their social skills from a distance.
endorsements	Recruiters assessed developers based on endorsements from others — such as followers on Twitter, forks on GitHub, or the things other developers said about a developer on social media.

B.1.6. Concept: Developer Scarcity

Recruiters observed a scarcity of desirable developers available for hire.

Code	Description
passionates scarce	Some recruiters said there was a scarcity of developers that are publicly involved and engaged.
personal network	Some recruiters utilized their personal networks.
access to personal network	Some recruiters said that the personal networks of developers — observable e.g. on LinkedIn — were a desirable asset to them.
OSS as reputation proxy	Some recruiters said they used the open source creations of developers and their dissemination in public as a reputation proxy.
authenticity	Some recruiters tried to maintain an authentic presence in social media to reach and assess developers, to stand out, and to overcome the bad reputation of recruiters among developers.

B.2. Category: Motivation

What are the different actors' reasons for participation in the social programmer ecosystem?

B.2.1. Concept: Passion

Developers were using social media because they allow them to follow their passions.

Code	Description
inspiration	Developers said that exposure to high-profile developers inspired them.
new tech	Developers were curios about new technology and liked to try out new things.
enjoyment	Developers thought the badges and the competition in social media — especially on Masterbranch and Coderwall — were fun.
learning	Developers were passionate to learn and liked to get feedback on their self-improvement.
become diverse	Developers used social media to become more diverse.

B.2.2. Concept: Assessment

Developers wanted to assess others and strived to improve their own visibility and appearance.

Code	Description
assessing others	Developers assessed other actors — companies, recruiters, and other developers.
visibility	Developers tried to improve their visibility with respect to recruiters and companies.
showing diversity	Developers strived to show diversity in their social media profiles.

186

B.2.3. Concept: Interaction with others

Developers said they liked interacting with others.

Code	Description
liking people	Developers liked connecting with and feeling related to interesting developers.
pride	Developers felt proud when their achievements were displayed on a social media site.
liking competition	Developers liked the competition, e.g. on the Coderwall leaderboard.
helping others	Developers liked helping other developers.
liking collaborating	Developers liked collaboration with other developers.
pushed by peers	Some developers used social media because their peers urged them to.
getting recognition	Some developers used social media to get recognized by the community.

B.2.4. Concept: Soft Skills

Recruiters were motivated to use social media for a deeper kind of assessment: one that would allow them find out more about the "softer" skills of developers.

Code	Description
identifying passionates	Recruiters tried to identify passionate and well-rounded developers.
identifying learners	Recruiters tried to identify developers that were able to adapt to new technologies.
identifying socials	Recruiters tried to identify socially adept developers.
completer picture	Recruiters tried getting a more complete picture of potential candidates.

B.2.5. Concept: Pressure to Hire

Recruiters were under a pressure to find potential candidates: developers as well as they time to find them were scarce.

Code	Description
active courting	Recruiters actively engaged with already otherwise employed developers because of the tight job market situation.
speed up hiring	Recruiters used social media to speed up finding new candidates.

B.3. Category: Problems

What problems do participants of the social programmer ecosystem encounter?

B.3.1. Concept: Pressure

Some developers felt overwhelmed by or left out of the social programmer ecosystem.

Code	Description
inferior	Some developers felt inferior in face of high-profile developers or felt being left out of the "in-crowd".
overwhelmed	Some developers felt overwhelmed by constantly having to keep up with new developments.
vocals	Some developers thought that there was too much focus on vocal high-profile developers in social media.

B.3.2. Concept: Reliability of signals

Many developers were aware that many social media signals might not be reliable.

Code	Description
hard to assess	Developers said that signal in social media were complicated to interpret, as the value of any reputation metric depends on the givers' reputations.
superficial	Developers though that social media signals were sometimes superficial, weak, or misleading.
manipulation	Developers were unsure about whether signal were manipulated and whether they should trust them.
backfiring	Developers thought that simplified quantifications such as badges on Coderwall might backfire, as people should rather scrutinize the actual code on GitHub, for example.
sensemaking	Developers were still in the process of sensemaking with regard to signals in social media.

B.3.3. Concept: Isolation

Some developers felt isolated from other communities, e.g. their local peers or certain groups in social media.

Code	Description
dislike aggression	Some developers disliked aggressive communities.
isolated locally	Some developers felt isolated locally.
recruiter chasm	Some developers acknowledged communication problems between developers and recruiters.

B.3.4. Concept: Reliability of Signals

Similar to developers, recruiters were also skeptical about the reliability of social media signals.

Code	Description
sensemaking	Some recruiters were still trying to make sense of the signals available in social media.
signal value	Some recruiters said there was questionable value in some of the signals in social media.
superficiality	Some recruiters said some of the social media signals were superficial.
manipulation	Some recruiters were worried whether social media signals could be manipulated and were unsure whether they should trust them.
north america	Some recruiters said the low adoption of social media signals outside of the US and Canada were a problem when trying to use them somewhere else.
fashion	Some recruiters thought there was a dangerous focus on short-lived fashions in social media.

B.3.5. Concept: Developer Scarcity

Recruiters encountered a set of problems related to the scarcity of developers in the job market.

Code	Description
soft skills wanted	Recruiters were looking to fulfill increasing requirements regarding soft skills.
no locals	Recruiters had problems finding developers locally.
traditional recruiting insufficient	Some recruiters acknowledged that more traditional recruiting strategies failed them.

B.3.6. Concept: Isolation

Recruiters would sometimes express that they felt disconnected or isolated from attractive developer communities.

Code	Description
not connected	Some recruiters felt that they were not connected to the developer community.
nontechnical chasm	Some recruiters acknowledged problems with non-technical recruiters trying to recruit technical candidates.
lonely innovator	Recruiters were aware that innovative employees might feel isolated within their companies.
unattractive location	Recruiters for companies in less attractive towns were struggling to attract talent.

B.3.7. Concept: Matchmaking

Recruiters either tried to use social media or avoided using them to find hires that would match a company's culture.

Code	Description
challenge tension	Some recruiters felt a tension between companies wanting "driven" developers and the possibly low attractiveness of a company's engineering problems.
mediation	External recruiters said that their role was one of mediation between developers and companies they were recruiting for.
OSS not for all	Some recruiters said that passion for open source in developers may not be appropriate for all companies.

B.4. Category: Impact

Which effects does participation in the social programmer ecosystem have on its members and their behaviors?

B.4.1. Concept: Enjoying Interactions

Developers said they enjoyed the interactions that social media allowed them to have with other developers.

Code	Description
enjoying community	Some developers felt excited about the developer community in social media and enjoyed it.
enjoying feedback	Developers enjoyed community feedback.
enjoying exposure	Developers enjoyed community exposure.
motivating others	Some developers were motivated to motivate peers.
enjoying competition	Developers enjoyed engaging in competition.
learning from others	Developers liked learning from others.
learning community norms	Developers used social media to learning the social norms of the community.

B.4.2. Concept: Assessment

Developers actively used and also provided signals that allowed them to assess and connect with other developers.

Code	Description
finding interesting peers	Developers used social media signals and quantified activity to find interesting peers.
becoming inspired by others	Developers used social media to be inspired by what other developers create.
showing diversity	Developers used social media to show their own diversity.
ambivalence towards signals	Developers felt ambivalent towards social media signals and quantified activity.

B.4.3. Concept: Job Finding

Whereas some developers had built up professional networks they said they could rely on should they need a new position, others said they were actively using social media to make themselves more attractive to recruiters.

Code	Description
own network for work	Some developers used their own professional networks for finding a job.
showing social skills	Some developers used social media to show their social skills to recruiters.
quantification for recruiters	Some developers engaged in social media to communicate better with recruiters and hoped to be better able to find a job through their activities there.
assessing companies	Developers used social media signals and quantified activity to assess companies.

B.4.4. Concept: Self-improvement

Many developers used signals and mechanisms from social media to support their own self-improvement.

Code	Description
enjoying feedback	Developers enjoyed quantified feedback on their own achievements.
self-improvement	Social media motivated developers to improve themselves.
more diversity	Social media motivated developers to become more diverse.
cosmopolite	Social media made developers feel more competent and cosmopolite.

B.4.5. Concept: Developer Scarcity

In face of the developer scarcity, recruiters said that social media allowed them to alleviate this to a degree.

Code	Description
access to developers	Recruiters felt social media provided them with easier access to good developers and let them become involved with them more easily.
candidates through OSS	Recruiters used social media to find candidates through their open source work.
candidates through personal network	Recruiters found candidates through their personal networks, sometimes supported by social media.

B.4.6. Concept: Assessment Accuracy

Some recruiters found that the social transparency in social media allowed them to more thoroughly assess developers, e.g. to get a feel for their personalities.

Code	Description
assessment through quantification	Recruiters felt they were able to create a more complete assessment of developers through quantified activity and that they were able to do so more easily.
social validation	Recruiters thought that assessment was easier through social validation available through social media.
assessing cultural fit	Recruiters felt that social media allowed them to assess cultural fit and social competence for developers.

B.4.7. Concept: Supporting Passion

Some companies actively used social media to support their employees' passions.

Code	Description
great company	Developers felt proud about their companies and liked that their companies' achievements were visible in social media.
employee motivation	Social media allowed employees of companies to motivate one another.
driving change	Developers said that participation in social media supported them in driving innovation and change in their companies.

B.4.8. Concept: Outside Assessment

Some companies used social media to improve their image for potential candidates.

Code	Description
company image	Internal recruiters felt that social media helped improving the perception of their companies by external developers.
company exposure	Internal recruiters felt that social media helped to open doors and increased exposure for their companies.

Curriculum Vitae

	Leif Singer
	born on September 16th 1979 in Hannover, Germany
Education	
04/2008–02/2013	Graduate Student in Computer Science, Leibniz Universität Hannover, Germany
10/2005–01/2008	Master of Science in Computer Science, Leibniz Universität Hannover, Germany
10/2002–09/2005	Bachelor of Science in Computer Science, Leibniz Universität Hannover, Germany
03/2001–08/2001	Apprenticeship Informatics Assistant Multimedia (aborted), b.i.b. e.V., Hannover, Germany
09/1986–05/1999	Abitur (general eligibility of university admission), Elementary School Pestalozzistrasse and Erich Kästner Gymnasium, Laatzen, Germany
Professional Experience	
04/2008–02/2013	Researcher at Software Engineering Group, Leibniz Universität Hannover, Germany
03/2006–03/2008	Student Assistant at Software Engineering Group, Leibniz Universität Hannover, Germany
05/2004–12/2005	Student Assistant at OptecNet Deutschland e.V. and Laserzentrum Hannover e.V., Hannover, Germany
08/2001–09/2002	Software Developer at A&L GmbH, Hannover, Germany
12/1999–01/2001	Co-Founder and Software Developer at wap3 Technologies GmbH, Cologne, Germany
08/1999–07/2000	Civil Service at Margarethenhof, Laatzen, Germany

Bibliography

[1] media. http://www.merriam-webster.com/dictionary/media, 2012. [Online; accessed Dec 1 2012]. 31

[2] M. Abdolrasulnia, B. Collins, L. Casebeer, T. Wall, C. Spettell, M. Ray, N. Weissman, and J. Allison. Using email reminders to engage physicians in an Internet-based CME intervention. *BMC medical education*, 4(1):17, 2004. 119

[3] N. Ahmadi, M. Jazayeri, F. Lelli, and S. Nesic. A survey of social software engineering. In *Automated Software Engineering - Workshops, 2008. ASE Workshops 2008. 23rd IEEE/ACM International Conference on*, pages 1 –12, sept. 2008. 39

[4] C. Alexander, S. Ishikawa, M. Silverstein, M. Jacobson, I. Fiksdahl-King, and S. Angel. *A Pattern Language: Towns, Buildings, Construction*. Oxford University Press, 1977. 91, 92

[5] A. Alvero, B. Bucklin, and J. Austin. An objective review of the effectiveness and essential characteristics of performance feedback in organizational settings (1985-1998). *Journal of Organizational Behavior Management*, 21(1):3–29, 2001. 130

[6] T. Amabile and S. Kramer. *The progress principle: Using small wins to ignite joy, engagement, and creativity at work*. Harvard Business Press, 2011. 2, 92, 109, 120, 121, 129, 169

[7] J. Antin and E. Churchill. Badges in Social Media: A Social Psychological Perspective. In *CHI 2011 Gamification Workshop Proceedings*, Vancouver, BC, Canada, 2011. 134, 135

[8] B. Balzer, M. Litoiu, H. Müller, D. Smith, M.-A. Storey, S. Tilley, and K. Wong. 4th International Workshop on Adoption-Centric Software Engineering. In *Proceedings of the 26th International Conference on Software Engineering (ICSE'04)*, 2004. 18

[9] A. Bandura. *Social Learning Theory*. Prentice Hall, Englewood Cliffs, New Jersey, USA, 1977. 10, 15, 115, 117, 136

[10] O. Barzilay. *Example Embedding: On the Diversity of Example Usage in Professional Software Development*. PhD thesis, Tel Aviv University, 2011. 127, 137

[11] V. R. Basili, G. Caldiera, and H. D. Rombach. The Experience Factory. In *Proceedings of the 14th annual Software Engineering Workshop*, 1989. 93

[12] S. Beecham, N. Baddoo, T. Hall, H. Robinson, and H. Sharp. Motivation in Software Engineering: A systematic literature review. *Information and Software Technology*, 50(9-10):860–878, 2008. 26

[13] A. Begel, R. DeLine, and T. Zimmermann. Social media for software engineering. In *Proceedings of the FSE/SDP workshop on Future of software engineering research*, FoSER '10, pages 33–38, New York, NY, USA, 2010. ACM. 39

[14] Y. Benkler. *The Penguin and the Leviathan: How Cooperation Triumphs over Self-Interest*. Random House, Inc., 2011. 117, 162, 163, 169

[15] D. Bertram, A. Voida, S. Greenberg, and R. Walker. Communication, collaboration, and bugs: the social nature of issue tracking in small, collocated teams. In *Proceedings of the 2010 ACM conference on Computer supported cooperative work*, CSCW '10, pages 291–300, New York, NY, USA, 2010. ACM. 3, 29, 38, 102

[16] B. Boehm. *Software engineering economics*. Prentice-Hall, 1981. 25

[17] B. W. Boehm and R. Ross. Theory-W Software Project Management Principles and Examples. *IEEE Trans. Softw. Eng.*, 15(7):902–916, July 1989. 165

[18] E. Bouwers, J. Visser, and A. van Deursen. Getting what you measure. *Communications of the ACM*, 55(7):54–59, 2012. 98, 132, 156

[19] G. Bowker and S. Star. *Sorting things out: classification and its consequences*. The MIT Press, Cambridge, MA, 2000. 72

[20] d. m. boyd and N. B. Ellison. Social Network Sites: Definition, History, and Scholarship. *Journal of Computer-Mediated Communication*, 13(1):210–230, 2007. 66

[21] Y. Brun, R. Holmes, M. D. Ernst, and D. Notkin. Proactive detection of collaboration conflicts. In *Proc. ESEC/FSE*, pages 168–178, 2011. 38, 139

[22] M. Burke, C. Marlow, and T. Lento. Feed me: motivating newcomer contribution in social network sites. In *Proc. CHI*, pages 945–954, 2009. 36, 115

[23] V. Bush. As We May Think. *Atlantic Monthly*, 176(1):101–108, July 1945. 29

[24] D. T. Campbell. Assessing the impact of planned social change. *Evaluation and Program Planning*, 2(1):67–90, 1979. 98, 114, 122, 123

[25] L. V. Casaló, J. Cisneros, C. Flavián, and M. Guinalíu. Reputation in Open Source Software Virtual Communities. In *Proc. IADIS International Conference e-Commerce*, 2008. 122

[26] D. Centola. The spread of behavior in an online social network experiment. *Science*, 329(5996):1194, 2010. 36, 103

[27] F. K. Chan and J. Y. Thong. Acceptance of agile methodologies: A critical review and conceptual framework. *Decision Support Systems*, 46(4):803–814, 2009. 42, 43

[28] C. Cheshire and J. Antin. The social psychological effects of feedback on the production of Internet information pools. *Journal of Computer-Mediated Communication*, 13(3):705–727, 2008. 121, 125

[29] J. Cohen. Modern Code Review. In A. Oram and G. Wilson, editors, *Making Software: What Really Works, and Why We Believe It*, pages 329–338. O'Reilly Media, Inc., 2010. 42

[30] J. Corbin and A. Strauss. *Basics of qualitative research: Techniques and procedures for developing grounded theory*. Sage Publications, 3rd edition, 2008. 74

[31] B. Cornelissen, A. Zaidman, A. van Deursen, L. Moonen, and R. Koschke. A Systematic Survey of Program Comprehension through

Dynamic Analysis. *Software Engineering, IEEE Transactions on*, 35(5):684 –702, 2009. 5

[32] J. Cranefield, P. Yoong, and S. Huff. Driving Change Through Brokering Practices In An Online Community Ecosystem. In *PACIS 2011 Proceedings*, 2011. 113

[33] J. W. Creswell and V. L. P. Clark. *Designing and Conducting Mixed Methods Research*. SAGE Publications, 2010. 4

[34] K. Crowston, K. Wei, Q. Li, and J. Howison. Core and periphery in Free/Libre and Open Source software team communications. In *Institute for Software Research*, page Paper 489, 2006. 60

[35] Csíkszentmihályi. *Flow: The Psychology of Optimal Experience*. Harper Perennial Modern Classics, 2008. 22

[36] R. Cuel, O. Morozova, M. Rohde, E. Simperl, K. Siorpaes, O. Tokarchuk, T. Wiedenhoefer, F. Yetim, and M. Zamarian. Motivation mechanisms for participation in human-driven semantic content creation. *International Journal of Knowledge Engineering and Data Mining*, 1(4):331–349, 2011. 163

[37] L. Dabbish, R. Farzan, R. Kraut, and T. Postmes. Fresh faces in the crowd: turnover, identity, and commitment in online groups. In *Proceedings of the ACM 2012 conference on Computer Supported Cooperative Work*, CSCW '12, pages 245–248, New York, NY, USA, 2012. ACM. 131

[38] L. Dabbish, C. Stuart, J. Tsay, and J. Herbsleb. Social coding in GitHub: transparency and collaboration in an open software repository. In *Proceedings of the ACM 2012 conference on Computer Supported Cooperative Work*, pages 1277–1286. ACM, 2012. 39, 45, 49, 67, 84, 158

[39] B. Dagenais and M. P. Robillard. Creating and evolving developer documentation: understanding the decisions of open source contributors. In *Proceedings of the eighteenth ACM SIGSOFT international symposium on Foundations of software engineering*, FSE '10, pages 127–136, New York, NY, USA, 2010. ACM. 39

[40] D. Damian, L. Izquierdo, J. Singer, and I. Kwan. Awareness in the wild: Why communication breakdowns occur. In *Second IEEE International Conference on Global Software Engineering*, pages 81–90. IEEE, 2007. 118, 131

[41] T. G. P. Davenport, editor. *Knowledge Management Case Book - Best Practises*. Publicis MCD, John Wiley & Sons, 2000. 164

[42] C. R. de Souza and D. Redmiles. The Awareness Network: To Whom Should I Display My Actions? And, Whose Actions Should I Monitor? In L. Bannon, I. Wagner, C. Gutwin, R. Harper, and K. Schmidt, editors, *ECSCW 2007*, pages 99–117. Springer London, 2007. 131

[43] E. Deci. Effects of externally mediated rewards on intrinsic motivation. *Journal of personality and Social Psychology*, 18(1):105–115, 1971. 22

[44] E. Deci and R. Ryan. *Handbook of self-determination research*. The University of Rochester Press, 2002. 21, 114, 119, 121, 122, 123, 164

[45] E. L. Deci, G. Betley, J. Kahle, L. Abrams, and J. Porac. When Trying to Win: Competition and Intrinsic Motivation. *Personality and Social Psychology Bulletin*, 7(1):79–83, 1981. 124

[46] T. DeMarco and T. Lister. *Peopleware*. Dorset House Pub., 1987. 26

[47] W. Deming. *Out of the Crisis*. MIT Press, 2000. 93

[48] S. Dencheva, C. R. Prause, and W. Prinz. Dynamic Self-moderation in a Corporate Wiki to Improve Participation and Contribution Quality. In *Proc. ECSCW*. Springer, New York, USA, 2011. 114, 121, 165

[49] S. Deterding. Gamification: designing for motivation. *interactions*, 19(4):14–17, July 2012. 164

[50] S. Deterding, D. Dixon, R. Khaled, and L. Nacke. From game design elements to gamefulness: defining "gamification". In *Proceedings of the 15th International Academic MindTrek Conference: Envisioning Future Media Environments*, MindTrek '11, pages 9–15, New York, NY, USA, 2011. ACM. 39, 40, 163

[51] P. Dourish and V. Bellotti. Awareness and coordination in shared workspaces. In *Proceedings of the 1992 ACM conference on*

Computer-supported cooperative work, CSCW '92, pages 107–114, New York, NY, USA, 1992. ACM. 33

[52] S. Draxler and G. Stevens. Supporting the Collaborative Appropriation of an Open Software Ecosystem. *Computer Supported Cooperative Work (CSCW)*, 20:403–448, 2011. 10.1007/s10606-011-9148-9. 81

[53] C. Dweck. *Mindset: The new psychology of success.* Ballantine Books, 2007. 126, 130

[54] C. A. Ellis, S. J. Gibbs, and G. Rein. Groupware: some issues and experiences. *Commun. ACM*, 34(1):39–58, Jan. 1991. 30

[55] N. B. Ellison and danah boyd. Sociality through Social Network Sites. In W. H. Dutton, editor, *The Oxford Handbook of Internet Studies (in press)*. Oxford University Press, 2013. 32, 46

[56] T. Erickson and W. A. Kellogg. Social translucence: an approach to designing systems that support social processes. *ACM Trans. Comput.-Hum. Interact.*, 7(1):59–83, Mar. 2000. 34, 67

[57] T. Erickson, D. N. Smith, W. A. Kellogg, M. Laff, J. T. Richards, and E. Bradner. Socially translucent systems: social proxies, persistent conversation, and the design of "babble". In *Proceedings of the SIGCHI conference on Human Factors in Computing Systems*, CHI '99, pages 72–79, New York, NY, USA, 1999. ACM. 34

[58] R. Farzan, J. M. DiMicco, D. R. Millen, C. Dugan, W. Geyer, and E. A. Brownholtz. Results from deploying a participation incentive mechanism within the enterprise. In *Proceedings of the SIGCHI Conference on Human Factors in Computing Systems*, CHI '08, pages 563–572, New York, NY, USA, 2008. ACM. 123

[59] J.-M. Favre, J. Estublier, and R. Sanlaville. Tool Adoption Issues in a Very Large Software Company. In *Proceedings of 3rd International Workshop on AdoptionCentric Software Engineering*, volume 9, pages 81–89, 2003. 102

[60] B. Fitzgerald. The use of systems development methodologies in practice: a field study. *Information Systems Journal*, 7(3):201–212, 1997. 42, 43

[61] B. Fitzgerald. An empirical investigation into the adoption of systems development methodologies. *Information & Management*, 34(6):317–328, 1998. 1, 42, 43

[62] B. J. Fogg. *Persuasive Technology: Using Computers to Change What We Think and Do.* Morgan Kaufmann, 2002. 2, 92, 118, 163

[63] B. J. Fogg. A behavior model for persuasive design. In *Proceedings of the 4th international Conference on Persuasive Technology*, page 40. ACM, 2009. 119, 128

[64] D. Foster, C. Linehan, B. Kirman, S. Lawson, and G. James. Motivating physical activity at work: using persuasive social media for competitive step counting. In *Proc. MindTrek*, pages 111–116. ACM, 2010. 115, 147

[65] J. Freyne, M. Jacovi, I. Guy, and W. Geyer. Increasing engagement through early recommender intervention. In *Proceedings of the third ACM conference on Recommender systems*, RecSys '09, pages 85–92, New York, NY, USA, 2009. ACM. 103

[66] D. Fudenberg and J. Tirole. *Game theory.* MIT Press, 1991. 163

[67] D. Funder. On the accuracy of personality judgment: a realistic approach. *Psychological review*, 102(4):652, 1995. 83

[68] M. Gagné and E. L. Deci. Self-determination theory and work motivation. *Journal of Organizational Behavior*, 26(4):331–362, 2005. 21

[69] E. Gamma, R. Helm, R. Johnson, and J. Vlissides. *Design Patterns - Elements of Reusable Object-Oriented Software.* Addison-Wesley Publishing Company, 1995. 42, 92

[70] E. Geller, T. Berry, T. Ludwig, R. Evans, M. Gilmore, and S. Clarke. A conceptual framework for developing and evaluating behavior change interventions for injury control. *Health Education Research*, 5(2):125–137, 1990. 2

[71] E. Gilbert. Designing social translucence over social networks. In *Proceedings of the 2012 ACM annual conference on Human Factors in Computing Systems*, CHI '12, pages 2731–2740, New York, NY, USA, 2012. ACM. 34, 35

[72] T. Gilbert. *Human Competence: Engineering Worthy Performance.* McGraw-Hill, 1978. 97

[73] A. Girgensohn and A. Lee. Making web sites be places for social interaction. In *Proceedings of the 2002 ACM conference on Computer supported cooperative work*, CSCW '02, pages 136–145, New York, NY, USA, 2002. ACM. 102

[74] E. Gleave, H. Welser, T. Lento, and M. Smith. A Conceptual and Operational Definition of 'Social Role' in Online Community. In *System Sciences, 2009. HICSS '09. 42nd Hawaii International Conference on*, pages 1 –11, jan. 2009. 67

[75] M. Godfrey and C. Kapser. Copy-Paste as a Principled Engineering Tool. In A. Oram and G. Wilson, editors, *Making Software: What Really Works, and Why We Believe It*, pages 531–544. O'Reilly Media, Inc., 2010. 127

[76] S. Goel, D. J. Watts, and D. G. Goldstein. The structure of online diffusion networks. In *Proceedings of the 13th ACM Conference on Electronic Commerce*, EC '12, pages 623–638, New York, NY, USA, 2012. ACM. 103

[77] A. Goldberg. Programmer as Reader. *IEEE Software*, 4:62–70, 1987. 41

[78] M. S. Granovetter. The Strength of Weak Ties. *American Journal of Sociology*, 78(6):1360–1380, May 1973. 14, 113

[79] M. Greiler, A. v. Deursen, and M.-A. Storey. Test confessions: a study of testing practices for plug-in systems. In *Proceedings of the 2012 International Conference on Software Engineering*, ICSE 2012, pages 244–254, Piscataway, NJ, USA, 2012. IEEE Press. 5

[80] J. Grudin. Computer-supported cooperative work: history and focus. *Computer*, 27(5):19–26, may 1994. 30, 33

[81] A. Guzzi and A. Begel. Facilitating communication between engineers with CARES. In *Proceedings of the 2012 International Conference on Software Engineering*, ICSE 2012, pages 1367–1370, Piscataway, NJ, USA, 2012. IEEE Press. 38, 102, 118

[82] A. M. Halavais. A Genealogy of Badges. *Information, Communication & Society*, 15(3):354–373, 2012. 115, 122, 134, 135

[83] J. Hamari and V. Eranti. Framework for designing and evaluating game achievements. *Proc. DiGRA 2011: Think Design Play*, 2011. 115, 122, 134, 135

[84] B. C. Hardgrave, F. D. Davis, and C. K. Riemenschneider. Investigating Determinants of Software Developers' Intentions to Follow Methodologies. *Journal of Management Information Systems*, 20(1):123–151, 2003. 1, 42, 43, 44

[85] J. Henrich, S. Heine, and A. Norenzayan. The weirdest people in the world? *Behavioral and Brain Sciences*, 33(2-3):61–83, 2010. 3, 110

[86] G. Hsieh, I. Li, A. Dey, J. Forlizzi, and S. E. Hudson. Using visualizations to increase compliance in experience sampling. In *Proceedings of the 10th international conference on Ubiquitous computing*, UbiComp '08, pages 164–167, New York, NY, USA, 2008. ACM. 120

[87] J. Iivari. Why are CASE tools not used? *Commun. ACM*, 39(10):94–103, Oct. 1996. 18

[88] J. Jung, C. Schneider, and J. Valacich. Enhancing the motivational affordance of information systems: The effects of real-time performance feedback and goal setting in group collaboration environments. *Management Science*, 56(4):724–742, 2010. 127, 131

[89] H. Kawasaki, A. Yamamoto, H. Kurasawa, H. Sato, M. Nakamura, and H. Matsumura. Top of worlds: method for improving motivation to participate in sensing services. In *Proceedings of the 2012 ACM Conference on Ubiquitous Computing*, UbiComp '12, pages 594–595, New York, NY, USA, 2012. ACM. 124

[90] J. H. Kietzmann, K. Hermkens, I. P. McCarthy, and B. S. Silvestre. Social media? Get serious! Understanding the functional building blocks of social media. *Business Horizons*, 54(3):241 – 251, 2011. 31

[91] A. J. Kim. *Building community on the Web: Secret strategies for successful online communities*. Peachpit Press, Berkeley, CA, 2000. 128

[92] B. Kitchenham. Procedures for Performing Systematic Reviews. Technical Report Keele University Technical Report TR/SE-0401, Software Engineering Group, Department of Computer Science, Keele University, 2004. 5, 107

[93] R. Kivetz, O. Urminsky, and Y. Zheng. The Goal-Gradient Hypothesis Resurrected: Purchase Acceleration, Illusionary Goal Progress, and Customer Retention. *Journal of Marketing Research*, 43(1):39–58, 2006. 129

[94] K. A. Kozar. Adopting Systems Development Methods: An Exploratory Study. *Journal of Management Information Systems*, 5(4):73–86, 1989. 43

[95] R. E. Kraut, P. Resnick, S. Kiesler, Y. Ren, Y. Chen, M. Burke, N. Kittur, J. Riedl, and J. Konstan. *Building Successful Online Communities: Evidence-Based Social Design*. The MIT Press, 2012. 161, 162, 169

[96] S. Kuznetsov. Motivations of contributors to Wikipedia. *SIGCAS Comput. Soc.*, 36(2), June 2006. 67

[97] I. Kwan and D. Damian. The hidden experts in software-engineering communication (NIER track). In *Proceedings of the 33rd International Conference on Software Engineering*, ICSE '11, pages 800–803, New York, NY, USA, 2011. ACM. 103

[98] C. Lampe and P. Resnick. Slash(dot) and burn: distributed moderation in a large online conversation space. In *Proceedings of the SIGCHI Conference on Human Factors in Computing Systems*, CHI '04, pages 543–550, New York, NY, USA, 2004. ACM. 133

[99] R. Landers and R. Callan. Casual Social Games as Serious Games: The Psychology of Gamification in Undergraduate Education and Employee Training. *Serious Games and Edutainment Applications*, pages 399–423, 2011. 98, 115, 122, 134, 135

[100] F. Lanubile, C. Ebert, R. Prikladnicki, and A. Vizcaino. Collaboration Tools for Global Software Engineering. *Software, IEEE*, 27(2):52–55, march-april 2010. 3, 37

[101] M. Lanza, L. Hattori, and A. Guzzi. Supporting Collaboration Awareness with Real-Time Visualization of Development Activity. In *14th European Conference on Software Maintenance and Reengineering (CSMR)*, pages 202–211, march 2010. 38

[102] M. Lavallée and P. N. Robillard. The impacts of software process improvement on developers: a systematic review. In *Proceedings of the 2012 International Conference on Software Engineering*, ICSE 2012, pages 113–122, Piscataway, NJ, USA, 2012. IEEE Press. 10, 42, 43, 120

[103] J. Lave and E. Wenger. *Situated learning: Legitimate peripheral participation*. Cambridge University Press, 1991. 60, 81

[104] J. Licklider and R. Taylor. The computer as a communication device. *Science and technology*, 76(2):2, 1968. 29

[105] O. Liechti. Awareness and the WWW: an overview. *SIGGROUP Bull.*, 21(3):3–12, Dec. 2000. 33

[106] A. Lih. Wikipedia as Participatory journalism: reliable sources? metrics for evaluating collaborative media as a news resource. In *In Proceedings of the 5th International Symposium on Online Journalism*, pages 16–17, 2004. 67

[107] K. Ling, G. Beenen, P. Ludford, X. Wang, K. Chang, X. Li, D. Cosley, D. Frankowski, L. Terveen, A. Rashid, P. Resnick, and R. Kraut. Using social psychology to motivate contributions to online communities. *Journal of Computer-Mediated Communication*, 10(4), 2005. 127

[108] E. A. Locke and G. P. Latham. Building a practically useful theory of goal setting and task motivation: A 35-year odyssey. *American Psychologist*, 57(9):705, 2002. 119, 122, 126, 128, 129, 130, 134, 135

[109] S. Lohmann, S. Dietzold, P. Heim, and N. Heino. A Web Platform for Social Requirements Engineering. In J. Münch and P. Liggesmeyer, editors, *Software Engineering (Workshops)*, volume 150 of *LNI*, pages 309–315. GI, 2009. 38

[110] C. López, R. Farzan, and P. Brusilovsky. Personalized incremental users' engagement: driving contributions one step forward. In

Proceedings of the 17th ACM international conference on Supporting group work, pages 189–198. ACM, 2012. 129

[111] J. Lou, K. H. Lim, Y. Fang, and J. Z. Peng. Drivers Of Knowledge Contribution Quality And Quantity In Online Question And Answering Communities. In *PACIS 2011 Proceedings*, 2011. 114

[112] P. Louridas. Using wikis in software development. *Software, IEEE*, 23(2):88 – 91, march-april 2006. 39

[113] F. C. Lunenburg. Goal-Setting Theory of Motivation. *International Journal of Management, Business, and Administration*, 15(1):1–6, 2011. 126, 130

[114] K. Luther, K. Caine, K. Ziegler, and A. Bruckman. Why it works (when it works): success factors in online creative collaboration. In *Proceedings of the 16th ACM international conference on Supporting group work*, GROUP '10, pages 1–10, New York, NY, USA, 2010. ACM. 109

[115] D. MacKenzie and J. Wajcman, editors. *The Social Shaping of Technology*. Open University Press, 2nd edition, 1999. 137, 168

[116] L. Mamykina, B. Manoim, M. Mittal, G. Hripcsak, and B. Hartmann. Design lessons from the fastest q&a site in the west. In *Proceedings of the 2011 annual conference on Human factors in computing systems*, pages 2857–2866. ACM, 2011. 39, 114, 115, 121

[117] A. Mazarakis and C. van Dinther. Feedback mechanisms and their impact on motivation to contribute to wikis in higher education. In *Proceedings of the 7th International Symposium on Wikis and Open Collaboration*, WikiSym '11, pages 215–216, New York, NY, USA, 2011. ACM. 124

[118] S. McConnell. Avoiding classic mistakes. *IEEE Software*, 13(5):111–112, 1996. 26

[119] M. McPherson, L. Smith-Lovin, and J. Cook. Birds of a feather: Homophily in social networks. *Annual review of sociology*, 27:415–444, 2001. 14

[120] L. A. Meyerovich and A. S. Rabkin. Socio-PLT: principles for programming language adoption. In *Proceedings of the ACM international symposium on New ideas, new paradigms, and reflections on programming and software*, Onward! '12, pages 39–54, New York, NY, USA, 2012. ACM. 161

[121] S. P. Mikawa, S. K. Cunnington, and S. A. Gaskins. Removing barriers to trust in distributed teams: understanding cultural differences and strengthening social ties. In *Proceedings of the 2009 international workshop on Intercultural collaboration*, IWIC '09, pages 273–276, New York, NY, USA, 2009. ACM. 37

[122] A. Monroy-Hernández, B. M. Hill, J. Gonzalez-Rivero, and d. boyd. Computers can't give credit: how automatic attribution falls short in an online remixing community. In *Proceedings of the SIGCHI Conference on Human Factors in Computing Systems*, CHI '11, pages 3421–3430, New York, NY, USA, 2011. ACM. 121

[123] M. Montola, T. Nummenmaa, A. Lucero, M. Boberg, and H. Korhonen. Applying game achievement systems to enhance user experience in a photo sharing service. In *Proceedings of the 13th International MindTrek Conference: Everyday Life in the Ubiquitous Era*, MindTrek '09, pages 94–97, New York, NY, USA, 2009. ACM. 123

[124] E. Murphy-Hill and G. Murphy. Peer interaction effectively, yet infrequently, enables programmers to discover new tools. In *Proceedings of the ACM 2011 conference on Computer supported cooperative work*, pages 405–414. ACM, 2011. 81

[125] N. Nagappan, E. Maximilien, T. Bhat, and L. Williams. Realizing quality improvement through test driven development: results and experiences of four industrial teams. *Empirical Software Engineering*, 13:289–302, 2008. 10.1007/s10664-008-9062-z. 90

[126] B. A. Nardi. *A Small Matter of Programming*. MIT Press, 1993. 81

[127] S. M. Nasehi, J. Sillito, F. Maurer, and C. Burns. What Makes a Good Code Example? A Study of Programming Q&A in StackOverflow. In *28th IEEE International Conference on Software Maintenance (ICSM)*, 2012. 127, 128

[128] S. Niebuhr and D. Kerkow. Captivating Patterns – A First Validation. In Y. Kort, W. IJsselsteijn, C. Midden, B. Eggen, and B. Fogg, editors, *Persuasive Technology*, volume 4744 of *Lecture Notes in Computer Science*, pages 48–54. Springer Berlin Heidelberg, 2007. 130

[129] J. C. Nunes and X. Drèze. The Endowed Progress Effect: How Artificial Advancement Increases Effort. *Journal of Consumer Research*, 32(4):pp. 504–512, 2006. 129

[130] R. Offen and R. Jeffery. Establishing software measurement programs. *Software, IEEE*, 14(2):45–53, mar/apr 1997. 44

[131] J. Olson, J. Howison, and K. Carley. Paying Attention to Each Other in Visible Work Communities: Modeling Bursty Systems of Multiple Activity Streams. In *2010 IEEE Second International Conference on Social Computing (SocialCom)*, pages 276 –281, Aug 2010. 131

[132] A. Oram and G. Wilson, editors. *Making Software: What Really Works, and Why We Believe It*. O'Reilly Media, Inc., 2010. 1

[133] D. Pagano and W. Maalej. How do developers blog?: an exploratory study. In *Proceedings of the 8th Working Conference on Mining Software Repositories*, MSR '11, pages 123–132, New York, NY, USA, 2011. ACM. 39, 114

[134] S. Park and F. Maurer. The role of blogging in generating a software product vision. In *Proceedings of the 2009 ICSE Workshop on Cooperative and Human Aspects on Software Engineering*, CHASE '09, pages 74–77, Washington, DC, USA, 2009. IEEE Computer Society. 39

[135] C. Parnin and S. Rugaber. Programmer information needs after memory failure. In *2012 IEEE 20th International Conference on Program Comprehension (ICPC)*, pages 123–132. IEEE, 2012. 119

[136] C. Parnin and C. Treude. Measuring API documentation on the web. In *Proceedings of the 2nd International Workshop on Web 2.0 for Software Engineering*, Web2SE '11, pages 25–30, New York, NY, USA, 2011. ACM. 39

[137] E. B. Passos, D. B. Medeiros, P. A. S. Neto, and E. W. G. Clua. Turning Real-World Software Development into a Game. In *SBC - Proceedings of SBGames 2011*, 2011. 164

[138] M. Peters. Konzeption und Implementierung eines erweiterbaren Digitalen Sozialen Netzwerks. Bachelorarbeit, Leibniz Universität Hannover, Fachgebiet Software Engineering, 9 2010. 101

[139] S. Pfleeger. Lessons learned in building a corporate metrics program. *Software, IEEE*, 10(3):67 –74, may 1993. 44

[140] R. Pham, L. Singer, O. Liskin, F. Figueira Filho, and K. Schneider. Creating a Shared Understanding of Testing Culture on a Social Coding Site. In *Proceedings of the 35th International Conference on Software Engineering (to appear)*, 2013. ii, 39, 45, 101, 112, 113, 127, 128, 137

[141] J. Preece and B. Shneiderman. The Reader-to-Leader Framework: Motivating technology-mediated social participation. *AIS Transactions on Human-Computer Interaction*, 1(1):13–32, 2009. 128

[142] R. Priedhorsky, J. Chen, S. T. K. Lam, K. Panciera, L. Terveen, and J. Riedl. Creating, destroying, and restoring value in wikipedia. In *Proceedings of the 2007 international ACM conference on Supporting group work*, GROUP '07, pages 259–268, New York, NY, USA, 2007. ACM. 67

[143] A. M. Rashid, K. Ling, R. D. Tassone, P. Resnick, R. Kraut, and J. Riedl. Motivating participation by displaying the value of contributions. In *Proceedings of the SIGCHI Conference on Human Factors in Computing Systems*, CHI '06, pages 955–958, New York, NY, USA, 2006. ACM. 120

[144] J. Reeve and E. L. Deci. Elements of the Competitive Situation that Affect Intrinsic Motivation. *Personality and Social Psychology Bulletin*, 22(1):24–33, 1996. 124

[145] M. Restivo and A. van de Rijt. Experimental Study of Informal Rewards in Peer Production. *PLoS ONE*, 7(3):e34358, 2012. 135

[146] C. Riemenschneider, B. Hardgrave, and F. Davis. Explaining software developer acceptance of methodologies: A comparison of five theoretical models. *IEEE Transactions on Software Engineering*, 28(12):1135–1145, 2002. 1, 42, 43, 44, 92

[147] K. Riemer, A. Richter, and P. Seltsikas. Enterprise Microblogging: Procrastination or productive use? In *AMCIS 2010 Proceedings*, 2010. 113

[148] P. Rigby, B. Cleary, F. Painchaud, M.-A. Storey, and D. German. Contemporary Peer Review in Action: Lessons from Open Source Development. *IEEE Software*, 29(6):56–61, Nov 2012. 132, 133

[149] E. M. Rogers. *Diffusion of Innovations*. Free Press, 5th edition, 2003. 1, 2, 4, 7, 8, 9, 10, 11, 12, 13, 14, 15, 16, 17, 18, 43, 62, 81, 85, 91, 96, 112, 113, 114, 116, 117, 118, 119, 120, 121, 123, 126, 127, 128, 131, 136, 137

[150] R. M. Ryan and E. L. Deci. Self-Determination Theory and the Facilitation of Intrinsic Motivation, Social Development, and Well-Being. *American Psychologist*, 51(1):68–78, 2000. 10, 21, 22, 23, 24, 25

[151] R. M. Ryan and E. L. Deci. Overview of self-determination theory: an organismic dialectical perspective. In E. L. Deci and R. M. Ryan, editors, *Handbook of self-determination research*, pages 3–33. University of Rochester Press, 2002. 21, 22

[152] R. Sach and M. Petre. Feedback: How does it impact software engineers? In *2012 5th International Workshop on Cooperative and Human Aspects of Software Engineering (CHASE)*, pages 129–131. IEEE, 2012. 26, 129

[153] R. Sach, H. Sharp, and M. Petre. Software Engineers' Perceptions of Factors in Motivation: The Work, People, Obstacles. In *International Symposium on Empirical Software Engineering and Measurement (ESEM)*, pages 368–371, 2011. 26

[154] M. J. Salganik, P. S. Dodds, and D. J. Watts. Experimental Study of Inequality and Unpredictability in an Artificial Cultural Market. *Science*, 311(5762):854–856, 2006. 117

[155] M. J. Salganik and D. J. Watts. Leading the Herd Astray: An Experimental Study of Self-fulfilling Prophecies in an Artificial Cultural Market. *Social Psychology Quarterly*, 71(4):338–355, 2008. 117

[156] K. Schneider. LIDs: A Light-Weight Approach to Experience Elicitation and Reuse. In F. Bomarius and M. Oivo, editors, *Product Focused Software Process Improvement*, volume 1840/2000 of *Lecture Notes in Computer Science*, pages 407–424. Springer, 2000. 104, 142

[157] D. Schuler and A. Namioka. *Participatory Design: Perspectives on Systems Design*. Taylor & Francis Group, 1993. 163

[158] P. Schultz, J. Nolan, R. Cialdini, N. Goldstein, and V. Griskevicius. The constructive, destructive, and reconstructive power of social norms. *Psychological Science*, 18(5):429–434, 2007. 117

[159] D. H. Schunk and C. W. Swartz. Goals and progress feedback: Effects on self-efficacy and writing achievement. *Contemporary Educational Psychology*, 18(3):337–354, 1993. 130

[160] A. J. Sellen, R. Murphy, and K. L. Shaw. How knowledge workers use the web. In *Proceedings of the SIGCHI Conference on Human Factors in Computing Systems*, CHI '02, pages 227–234, New York, NY, USA, 2002. ACM. 102

[161] C. Shah and G. Marchionini. Awareness in collaborative information seeking. *Journal of the American Society for Information Science and Technology*, 61(10):1970–1986, 2010. 34

[162] L. Singer, F. F. Filho, B. Cleary, C. Treude, M.-A. Storey, and K. Schneider. Mutual Assessment in the Social Programmer Ecosystem: An Empirical Investigation of Developer Profile Aggregators. In *Proceedings of the ACM 2013 conference on Computer Supported Cooperative Work and Social Computing (in press)*, CSCW '13, New York, NY, USA, 2013. ACM. ii, 35, 36, 40, 66, 121, 122, 134, 135

[163] L. Singer and M. Peters. Hallway: ein Erweiterbares Digitales Soziales Netzwerk. In R. Reussner, M. Grund, A. Oberweis, and W. Tichy, editors, *Software Engineering 2011*, volume P-183 of *Lecture Notes in Informatics (LNI) — Proceedings*, pages 147–158, Bonn, 2011. Gesellschaft für Informatik. 101

[164] L. Singer and K. Schneider. It was a Bit of a Race: Gamification of Version Control. In *Proceedings of the 2nd international workshop on Games and software engineering*, 2012. 99, 154

[165] R. Spier. The history of the peer-review process. *Trends in Biotechnology*, 20(8):357–357, 2002. 132

[166] K. Stapel and K. Schneider. Managing Knowledge on Communication and Information Flow in Global Software Projects. *Expert Systems*, Special Issue on Knowledge Engineering in Global Software Development, 2012. 29

[167] K. Stein and C. Hess. Does it matter who contributes: a study on featured articles in the german wikipedia. In *Proceedings of the eighteenth conference on Hypertext and hypermedia*, HT '07, pages 171–174, New York, NY, USA, 2007. ACM. 67

[168] I. Steinmacher, A. P. Chaves, and M. A. Gerosa. Awareness Support in Distributed Software Development: A Systematic Review and Mapping of the Literature. *Computer Supported Cooperative Work (CSCW)*, pages 1–46, 2012. 37

[169] M.-A. Storey, C. Treude, A. van Deursen, and L.-T. Cheng. The impact of social media on software engineering practices and tools. In *Proceedings of the FSE/SDP workshop on Future of software engineering research*, FoSER '10, pages 359–364, New York, NY, USA, 2010. ACM. 2, 39

[170] A. Strauss and J. Corbin. *Grounded Theory in Practice*. SAGE Publications, 1997. 4, 5, 46, 47, 108

[171] H. C. Stuart, L. Dabbish, S. Kiesler, P. Kinnaird, and R. Kang. Social transparency in networked information exchange: a theoretical framework. In *Proceedings of the ACM 2012 conference on Computer Supported Cooperative Work*, CSCW '12, pages 451–460, New York, NY, USA, 2012. ACM. 35, 47, 67, 80, 83

[172] B. Suh, E. H. Chi, A. Kittur, and B. A. Pendleton. Lifting the veil: improving accountability and social transparency in Wikipedia with wikidashboard. In *Proceedings of the twenty-sixth annual SIGCHI conference on Human factors in computing systems*, CHI '08, pages 1037–1040, New York, NY, USA, 2008. ACM. 67

[173] A. Sukumaran, S. Vezich, M. McHugh, and C. Nass. Normative influences on thoughtful online participation. In *Proceedings of the*

SIGCHI Conference on Human Factors in Computing Systems, CHI '11, pages 3401–3410, New York, NY, USA, 2011. ACM. 116

[174] M. Sulayman and E. Mendes. A Systematic Literature Review of Software Process Improvement in Small and Medium Web Companies. In D. Ślęzak, T.-h. Kim, A. Kiumi, T. Jiang, J. Verner, and S. Abrahão, editors, *Advances in Software Engineering*, volume 59 of *Communications in Computer and Information Science*, pages 1–8. Springer Berlin Heidelberg, 2009. 42

[175] E. Sun, I. Rosenn, C. Marlow, and T. Lento. Gesundheit! modeling contagion through facebook news feed. In *Proceedings of the International AAAI Conference on Weblogs and Social Media*, 2009. 103

[176] K. Sylwester and G. Roberts. Cooperators benefit through reputation-based partner choice in economic games. *Biology Letters*, 6(5):659–662, 2010. 114, 122

[177] J. M. Tauer and J. M. Harackiewicz. Winning Isn't Everything: Competition, Achievement Orientation, and Intrinsic Motivation. *Journal of Experimental Social Psychology*, 35(3):209–238, 1999. 124, 125

[178] J. Thom, D. R. Millen, and J. DiMicco. Removing Gamification from an Enterprise SNS. In *Proc. CSCW*. ACM, 2012. 104, 123

[179] W. Tichy. The Evidence for Design Patterns. In A. Oram and G. Wilson, editors, *Making Software: What Really Works, and Why We Believe It*, pages 393–414. O'Reilly Media, Inc., 2010. 42

[180] C. Treude and M. Storey. Awareness 2.0: Staying aware of projects, developers and tasks using dashboards and feeds. In *Proc. ICSE*, 365–374. ACM, 2010. 37

[181] B. Turhan, L. Layman, M. Diep, H. Erdogmus, and F. Shull. How Effective Is Test-Driven Development? In A. Oram and G. Wilson, editors, *Making Software: What Really Works, and Why We Believe It*, pages 207–219. O'Reilly Media, Inc., 2010. 42

[182] M. Umarji and C. Seaman. Predicting acceptance of Software Process Improvement. *SIGSOFT Softw. Eng. Notes*, 30(4):1–6, May 2005. 44

[183] R. Vallerand, S. Salvy, G. Mageau, A. Elliot, P. Denis, F. Grouzet, and C. Blanchard. On the role of passion in performance. *Journal of Personality*, 75(3):505–534, 2007. 82

[184] R. J. Vallerand and G. Reid. On the causal effects of perceived competence on intrinsic motivation: A test of cognitive evaluation theory. *Journal of Sport Psychology*, 6(1):94–102, 1984. 22

[185] R. van Solingen and E. Berghout. *The Goal/Question/Metric Method: A Practical Guide for Quality Improvement of Software Development.* McGraw-Hill Publishing Company, 1999. 94, 96, 98

[186] D. VandeWalle, W. L. Cron, and J. W. Slocum Jr. The role of goal orientation following performance feedback. *Journal of Applied Psychology*, 86(4):629–640, Aug 2001. 130

[187] Vereinigung Cockpit e.V. Ryanair bedroht spanischen Pilotenverband, press release, Sep 10 2012. 124

[188] A. Vermeulen, S. Ambler, G. Bumgardner, E. Metz, T. Misfeldt, J. Shur, and P. Thompson. *The Elements of Java (TM) Style*, volume 15. Cambridge University Press, 2000. 42

[189] G. M. Walton, G. L. Cohen, D. Cwir, and S. J. Spencer. Mere belonging: The power of social connections. *Journal of Personality and Social Psychology*, 102(3):513–532, Mar 2012. 124

[190] Y. Wang, W. Gräther, and W. Prinz. Suitable notification intensity: the dynamic awareness system. In *Proceedings of the 2007 international ACM conference on Supporting group work*, pages 99–106. ACM, 2007. 34, 119, 131, 132

[191] K. Werbach and D. Hunter. *For the Win: How Game Thinking Can Revolutionize Your Business.* Wharton Digital Press, 2012. 164

[192] L. Williams. Pair Programming. In A. Oram and G. Wilson, editors, *Making Software: What Really Works, and Why We Believe It*, pages 311–328. O'Reilly Media, Inc., 2010. 42

[193] R. K. Wilson and J. Sell. "Liar, Liar...": Cheap Talk and Reputation in Repeated Public Goods Settings. *The Journal of Conflict Resolution*, 41(5):695–717, 1997. 125

[194] S. S. Wiltermuth and F. Gino. "I'll Have One of Each": How Separating Rewards into (Meaningless) Categories Increases Motivation. *Journal of Personality and Social Psychology*, (in press), 2013. 134, 135

[195] C. Wu, J. Gerlach, and C. Young. An empirical analysis of open source software developers' motivations and continuance intentions. *Information & Management*, 44(3):253–262, 2007. 82

[196] Y. Ye and K. Kishida. Toward an understanding of the motivation of open source software developers. In *Proceedings of the 25th International Conference on Software Engineering*, pages 419–429, 2003. 84

[197] H. Zhu, R. Kraut, and A. Kittur. Organizing without formal organization: group identification, goal setting and social modeling in directing online production. In *Proceedings of the ACM 2012 conference on Computer Supported Cooperative Work*, CSCW '12, pages 935–944, New York, NY, USA, 2012. ACM. 127

[198] M. Zuckerman, J. Porac, D. Lathin, and E. L. Deci. On the Importance of Self-Determination for Intrinsically-Motivated Behavior. *Personality and Social Psychology Bulletin*, 4(3):443–446, 1978. 22